No, I Live Here

No, I Live Here

To Robin
with best wishes,
Sylvia Jones
Oct. 2006

Sylvia Jones

dinas

Acknowledgements

Our thanks to the staff at Y Lolfa for making this project a reality and to all our family and friends for their encouragement in so many ways, especially those most directly involved: Julie Freeman in California; Rhodri Clark, Gill Anstis, C.A. Lister, and Llew Groom in Wales. We are grateful to the Welsh Slate Museum at Llanberis for permission to use quotations.

Photo Credits

All photos by Peter Jones

except: 'Jake' by Alan Naughton (p.34); '11th October' by Rhodri Clark (p.87); 'Gwilym' (p.22), 'Flood' (p.28), 'Ewe' (p.70), and 'Jocan', page 94 by the author.

Cover photo: on Pen y Gaer
overlooking the lower Conwy Valley, by Peter Jones

Peter George Jones

Dinas is an imprint of Y Lolfa

ISBN: 0 86243 858 6

Printed and published in Wales
by Y Lolfa Cyf., Talybont, Ceredigion SA24 5AP
e-mail ylolfa@ylolfa.com
website www.ylolfa.com
tel. (01970) 832304
fax (01970) 832782

*It's the same everywhere I go — in shops, an ice cream stand
on the quay, chatting with people on the streets.
They hear my accent and ask, "Are you on holiday?"
"No, I live here," I say, with pleasure and pride.
Depending on the circumstances, sometimes I give a brief
explanation, but this is the whole story of falling in love with Wales
and a Welshman.*

Chapter One

Mince Pies by the Fireside

It was his pre-dawn gesture, a week before Christmas, which hooked me. Without that, it's possible I might have avoided making a fool of myself, feeling like a smitten teenager at the ripe age of fifty-seven.

We'd met the evening before at a small, quiet Christmas social, where we talked for two hours; my only reaction then was surprise at meeting a Welshman with whom I had so much in common. But the next morning, when the dog and I approached the front door, I found an envelope on the floor below the letterbox.

"It's awfully early for the Post," I said to Gwilym, and then realized there was no stamp or address on the envelope. Puzzled and intrigued, I made the poor dog wait while I opened and read the little Christmas card. The lovely, brief message written in a strong masculine hand hopelessly captivated my imagination. They were only words of friendship, but it was such an original and charming thing to have done at five o'clock on a winter's morning.

"This is a special guy – a one-off, as you say over here," I explained to Gwilym.

My association with Conwy had begun nearly six years before – in March 1996, on the Marine Walk. Very few strollers were out in the bitter wind that tossed a flurry of snow in my face and made me shiver inside my coat. Walking toward me were a woman and a large, unusual-looking dog that came bounding up to me. Petting Gwilym, I chatted with his companion but soon suggested we keep walking while we talked, "Because I'm from California and not used to this cold wind." So Mona invited me to her nearby home for tea. While I sat in a comfortable chair, Gwilym stood up and put his front paws on my shoulders and looked me in the eye.

"Are you going to be our friend?" he seemed to be asking.

The answer was definitely, "Yes!"

In the following years, Mona and I visited each other in Conwy and in the San Francisco suburbs. It was always a pleasure to return to Conwy and to get to know Mona and Gwilym better.

Speaking to Mona on the phone in the summer of 2001, I told her my life was at a crossroads, and that I was definitely leaving California but didn't know where I was going from there.

"I think I'll take six months in Britain, to sort myself out before deciding."

When I told Mona I was aiming for autumn in Scotland and winter in Wales, she said she'd be gone part of the winter, visiting family in the States.

"I'm worried about leaving Gwilly in a kennel for two months, at his age, though."

Off the top of my head, I volunteered to dog-sit.

After two-and-a-half months in the Borders of Scotland, I arrived in Conwy on the seventh of December. Mona and I had a few days together before she flew off for an extended Christmas holiday, and then the reality hit me. Christmas was only a fortnight away, and the only person I knew in this town had just left the country. Of course, I'd known when I made the arrangements that it meant spending Christmas on my own, except for Gwilym, but it was months away then, and I told myself I could deal with it when the time came. There had been plenty of other things to occupy my mind as I eliminated possessions, put the remaining things in storage, and said goodbye to many friends, while preparing to go to meet my unknown future. My departure was complicated by the fact that it was just a fortnight after the horrific 9/11 terrorist attacks in New York, and I didn't know if my scheduled flight would be going, or if it was even appropriate for me to begin my personal odyssey when so many people were suffering such terrible losses. Friends convinced me there was nothing I could do to help, and the airline said the flight would go as planned. So I found myself facing Christmas alone for the first time in my life.

Frequenting the Conwy library to check my e-mail, I saw many notices on the wall about Christmas activities, and I took notes and made some tentative plans. First on my list was ringing Conwy Camera Club, but the information was disappointing: the next meeting was a Christmas social and then there'd be a break until the fifteenth of January. The pleasant young man on the line assured me I'd be welcome at the party, but I said I didn't think I'd want to do that. Having the courage to ring him at all was largely due to a woman I'd met in Galashiels, at the recommendation of a mutual friend in California. Hearing about her local meetings and competitions dispelled the notion that a camera club must be a stuffy group of men sitting around and discussing technical details. But crashing their Christmas party was a different matter entirely.

The Conwy Town Band's Christmas concert was another forthcoming event I wrote down at the library, and it proved to be an excellent evening. When the audience sang the beautiful Welsh National Anthem with such spirit at the end, I vowed to be able to sing along next time I was in such a situation.

Carol services at two churches went onto my list as well, and the thought of attending St. Mary's Church again brought back memories of an evening service in Welsh during my first visit to Conwy. I had spoken to the clergyman outside, and he was very welcoming, in spite of my not understanding the language. There were only twelve of us, and we sat in the choir, men and women on opposite sides. The hymn tunes were unfamiliar to me, but they rendered them beautifully. Taking in our surroundings as I listened to the Welsh singing, I admired the woodwork and the effect of daylight slowly fading from the stained glass windows, casting a solemnity over everything. The first hymn was in a sombre, minor key, and I kept glancing down the nave, expecting to see a procession of hooded monks approaching the altar. And then there was the sermon. If you've ever thought the preacher was speaking directly to you, you haven't really experienced that until he translates the most important points, just for you! No doubt at a carol service I would be quite inconspicuous and understand much more.

Mingling with shoppers, I took in the festive Saturdays on the High Street as Father Christmas and the Town Crier wandered about, creating a holiday mood.

Familiar from previous trips, looming, thirteenth-century Conwy Castle and its town walls made an interesting contrast as a backdrop to colourful Christmas decorations. Cutting through St. Mary's churchyard, checking the time on her chiming clock, or taking in the sights on the streets and quay, brought back happy memories of my earlier trips, when I was able to visit Plas Mawr – an Elizabethan town house, Aberconwy House – a fifteenth-century merchant's dwelling and shop, and the Smallest House in Britain, all of which were now closed for the winter. But just living with the exteriors of these fascinating buildings was enriching. I remembered a description in an old book:

'Now I, too, had come to stop as long as possible.'
Conwy Castle from across the estuary

> … I always visit Conway and stop as long as possible in its quaint and ancient streets and by the old quay with the towers of the great palace of the Normans above. (*Odd Corners in North Wales* by William T. Palmer, 1946).

Now I, too, had come to "…stop as long as possible."

On the eighteenth, I changed my mind many times, but in the end, thinking, "What have I got to lose?" I went to the Camera Club Christmas party.

I'd been sitting and chatting for about fifteen minutes when a tall, curly-haired, blue-eyed man walked in, casually dropped a bag of mince pies onto the table, and sat down across from me. I soon learned that his name was Peter and that he was late because he'd just finished his shift as a local bus driver. That he'd made the mince pies he brought was revealed later. We talked about photography, hiking, classical music, and my previous trips to Britain, discovering that, after our mutual love of Wales, we also shared an interest in Scotland, along with similar tastes in most things. He told of his previous career in civil engineering, including a year in the Lake District and another year in Shetland. My former jobs in Sequoia National Park visitor centres and offices, and especially the hiking I'd done there, were of great interest to him.

Having exchanged phone numbers and addresses, we said goodbye with a tentative plan that he'd show me around on Boxing Day. I walked back to Mona's alone and took Gwilym out for his last stroll, thinking about my new acquaintance with interest.

An unusually early shift the next morning gave Peter the opportunity to drop the Christmas card through Mona's door while Gwilym and I slept upstairs – that move that would pique my interest so much more. For the next few days, I wondered if he would ring to firm up the Boxing Day plan; he did, on the twenty-second.

Two nearby trips on my own gave me pleasure during those pre-Christmas days. My first bus trip was to Llandudno, a popular Victorian resort that had developed near the site of an ancient copper-mining village. I walked the Promenade and along sand dunes on the West Shore on a bright, clear day. A famous hotel was originally a residence belonging to the Lidell family, and folklore claims that Lewis Carroll visited them here and used local settings for *Alice in Wonderland*. Some writers, however, cast doubt on his ever having visited Wales, but since Alice really did live here, that at least makes the legend possible, if not certain.

Walking along a busy road to Conwy Nature Reserve, created by the Royal Society for the Protection of Birds (RSPB), using material excavated in the construction of the Conwy tunnel in 1991, I passed a multi-screen cinema and several American fast-food establishments. When I'd finished seeing the Reserve, so near yet so far from all the commercial busy-ness, I really appreciated what had been done in making this waterfowl area beside the estuary. Heavy skies did not dampen my enthusiasm for views of attractive reed beds backed by waterways and layers of hills. It wasn't an ideal time for bird watching, but I enjoyed the ducks and geese. Easy trails and hides overlooking the lagoons, with views of the bridges and castle not far away, made this an area I planned to keep revisiting.

That Sunday I joined in the carol services at St. Mary's in the morning and St. John's in the evening. Both were wonderful – the first featuring several excellent choir selections, and the second, all congregational singing with pleasing instrumental accompaniment. I recognised the euphonium player from the Town Band concert. Walking home in light rain, I was still singing, *O tidings of comfort and joy*.

'It was on the afternoon of the day of Christmas Eve' that I listened to a tape of Dylan Thomas reading *A Child's Christmas in Wales*, which the library staff had found for me before closing for the holidays. After watching *The Snowman* on the television, I walked to Lancaster Square, where a crowd of families gathered around the Town Band and the tree decked in red and white lights. The day had been mild, and even with a strong wind in the evening, it wasn't terribly cold as we stood and sang carols. Having been led to the castle car park by the Band, the crowd looked up at the floodlit towers. It must have been thrilling for youngsters, because even I felt a jolt of pleasure at the sight of the red-suited, white-bearded figure making his way across the ramparts, waving to the crowd. Red and green fireworks exploded over the towers to conclude the evening's events. *'No one could have had a noisier Christmas Eve.'*

The wind persisted on Christmas morning, but the temperature had dropped. After opening my presents, I took Gwilym for a longer walk, and as he sniffed around in the grass behind the castle, I watched clouds thicken and darken. When I felt a few tentative drops, I spread my black-mittened hands hopefully – and, yes! It was snowing on Christmas morning. When we headed home, I stepped briefly into the news agent's shop to wish George a Happy Christmas. No one else was out on the High Street.

A Christmas dinner of turkey sandwich and mince slice, procured the day before, was followed by a walk among the holly and the ivy in Bodlondeb Wood, Gwil's favourite walk. The carol countdown on Classic FM, the Queen's speech on the television, and several trans-Atlantic phone calls got me through Christmas day. '*And then I went to bed. … I said some words to the close and holy darkness, and then I slept.*'

My first Boxing Day brought intermittent, sleety, snow showers, and Nature baited the trap being set for me with a most evocative scene. Since I'd grown up in the Eastern US but spent most of my adult life in California, snow held a strong nostalgic charm for me. At Bwlch-y-Ddeufaen above Rowen, Peter and I walked in the snow and bitter wind, and I revelled in the crunch of snow underfoot, the perfectly packable snow that produced the snowball I lobbed at my new companion, and the delicate sunset over Snowdonia, living up to its name.

Peter had given me lunch at the Lodge in Tal y Bont, and, after our snowy trip, we had tea at his place, followed by more of his homemade mince pies by the fireside. What a natural romantic, I thought, even as I realized there was no hint of romance in his attitude toward me.

On the thirtieth, when I spoke with him after the morning service at St. John's, he spontaneously asked if I'd like to go to see another snowy viewpoint, and I accepted. Following lunch in the Queen's Head, Glanwyddan, we went to Nant-y-Gamar above Llandudno. On a slope between the estuary and Snowdonia's long white ridge perched the ancient walled town of Conwy with its massive grey castle, looking like a scene in a storybook. Snow lay around us, and the cold, windy day was drawing in with another ethereal sunset.

'The ancient walled town... like a scene in a story book...'
The view from Nant-y-Gamar at a brighter time of year

Chapter Two

Blwyddyn Newydd Dda!

"For someone who isn't interested in me, Peter certainly doesn't seem to mind my company!" I told Gwilym, apologising for leaving him on his own again. Peter had invited me to join him and two friends for a New Year's Day trip, and he picked me up at ten in the morning.

Before his two friends arrived, Peter took me to meet his brother, John, sister-in-law, Gwen, and their little dog, Honey. We had an enjoyable visit that left me wondering how much more I would see of them and if there was any significance to his introducing me to his family.

The spectacular drive with Tony and Gretta made for a most memorable day, and I enjoyed getting to know them. Tony, a long-term colleague of Peter's, is tall, thin, with closely-cropped, greying hair and a studious expression. Runner, mountain-climber, and amateur astronomer, he is an Englishman who is fluent in Welsh and French and easily picks up a bit of any language that comes to his attention, sometimes thanking foreign visitors on his bus in anything from Polish to Shona. Gretta, his wife, who comes from the North of Ireland, is delightful company, and I was comfortable with both of them from the start.

Between Betws-y-Coed and Capel Curig, our first stop was Cyfyng Falls, where the shadow of the hill and the freezing temperatures created a black and white scene of granite, dark

'Coppery grasses added to the rich colour scheme...'
Llynnau Mymbyr

pools, and curtains of icicles suspended from the rocky overhang on the far side of the river. Huge rocks form islands in the River Llugwy, and saplings have sprouted in them, along with the lichens that provided the first fragments of soil for a progression of plants to colonise. Some of the water was still free to fall in cascades and over shelves, diverted into small rocky pools that are cut off in low water but fill and spill when the flow is greater. Above the falls stands the rustic arch of Pont Cyfyng, a narrow stone bridge that was built of local granite to carry the road, many years ago, in the days when the only traffic would have been horses and carts and the occasional stagecoach.

Llynnau Mymbyr presented brighter opportunities for photographs, with their pale blue, frozen surface, and concentric circles artistically etched in the ice around the bases of the rust-coloured rocks that border the lakes. Coppery grasses added to the rich colour scheme, and grey rocks showed through on the snow-covered mountains, their southern flanks highlighted by the late-morning sun. Peter told me that the curved Snowdon massif is known locally as the Snowdon Horseshoe. Mt. Snowdon's classic pointed profile was familiar to me because Mona had taken me up on the mountain railway in 1999, but I'd never seen this highest of the Welsh peaks adorned in snow.

Backtracking to Capel Curig, we followed the River Llugwy towards Llyn Ogwen, where we stopped by the roadside to take photographs of the lake. Tony suggested he take one of Peter and me, with my camera, and when we awkwardly stood a little bit apart, he urged us to get closer. Laughing and throwing caution to the wind, I took Peter's arm and stood quite close. Tony snapped a momentous first photo of us by the frozen, one-mile-long lake attractively nestled below the snowy slopes of the Glyders and precipitous, fin-shaped Tryfan.

Our route continued down the Nant Francon Pass, where the River Ogwen tumbled over rocks before winding across the flat valley floor, with rugged, snow-covered mountain slopes rising steeply on either side. We could only imagine the forces of moving ice that had carved out this glacial valley. A handsome group of Scots pines stood by the road, and trees and shrubs grew on huge slate tips that have been there long enough to allow substantial purchase for their roots, and the valley closed in as we approached Bethesda.

Born out of the local slate quarrying industry, the town, with its narrow streets and slate-roofed, terraced houses, felt confining after such beautiful wild scenery. Its biblical name came from its chapel on the main street, which is nicely painted and well kept up. Although the building still bears the old announcement boards, they now proclaim only that it was built in 1820, renovated in 1840, and reopened as flats in 1998.

After crossing Britannia Bridge to the island of Anglesey, we stopped at the viewpoint overlooking the Menai Straits and Telford's suspension bridge, a place that stands out in my memory, not because of its scenic charms, but because I closed the car door on Tony's fingers! Dying a thousand deaths of remorse and embarrassment as I watched him suffer in silence, I hoped the time for first impressions was already passed. I am surprised to find I took a pleasing photo of the view after my clumsy accident; I suppose I didn't know what else to do with myself after apologising profusely, so I busied myself with my camera.

Mona had also taken me to see Beaumaris Castle during my 1999 visit, but that was all I'd ever seen of the island. Just outside Llanfair P.G., famous for its long name, Peter headed southwest to Newborough. The "new" in Newborough goes back seven hundred years, to the time when Edward I relocated the inhabitants of Llanfaes so that he could build Beaumaris Castle nearby. A new borough was created for the displaced population, and it went on to become an important market town. We turned in the middle of the village and drove through the forestry, paying a toll of two pounds to enter. In *Odd Corners in North Wales*, William Palmer talks about how, in the 1940s, many scenic areas had to rely on tolls for their upkeep, and this may be a carryover from that scheme. With a background of thirty-four miles of Snowdonia's glistening white peaks, the tide-rippled golden sands of Newborough beach were a delight. Then it was time to go home and take care of the very patient and forgiving Gwilym. Except for the accident with the car door, it had been a glorious day in very pleasant company.

A few days later, Peter took me for a hilly walk on the south side of Sychnant Pass.

> Perhaps the most startling change of scenery in North Wales is the Sychnant Pass that connects Conway with Penmaenmawr. In the twinkling of an eye you leave the friendly scenery of a river estuary and find yourself plunged into a miniature mountain gorge as grim in its way as anything in Scotland.

So H. V. Morton described it in 1932, in his famous work, a favourite among my old British books: *In Search of Wales*. I found the area very appealing.

At nine hundred feet elevation, we looked down on the pass that skirts a deep, dry chasm. The hillsides around here and nearby Conwy Mountain are patchworks of gorse, heather, and grey rocks, perhaps 'grim' in winter colours. I did wish to see them in late summer, when the heather would add its bright purple to the nearly year-round yellow of gorse. There aren't many extensive tracts of heather remaining in Snowdonia because sheep have a huge impact on the plant, unless it grows in places too steep to be grazed, or where sheep are kept out. At any rate, seeing Conwy Mountain in bloom would have to wait.

Fairy Glen near Betws-y-Coed was our destination on the twelfth of January, where we walked a woodland trail bordered by ash and oaks, and relished the sound of the Conwy River below. At the bottom, we stood by the riverside, where fishermen's shelters on each side of a slow, wide stretch conjured up visions of quiet, summer evenings and a solitary angler stalking these banks in search of the perfect salmon pool. Then we climbed away from the river again and came upon a stand of silver birch trees, elegant in the soft, slanted light of early afternoon. Sitting on a bench, we gazed at a view of the river framed by a twisted, gnarled oak and a leaning, ivy-covered ash tree. A moss-covered tree with a shattered top held a miniature garden of ferns and ivy on a wide horizontal limb.

Down the slippery granite steps we climbed and ventured onto even more slippery rocks beside the ebullient Conwy as it splashed over boulders sculpted by centuries of snow-melt and storm–spate. Here the gorge is so steep and narrow that the sun is unable to reach the bottom during the shortest days of winter. Patches of ice clung to the edges of some of the rocks, but the water reflected the green of the walls. One could almost believe in fairies and leprechauns in these enchanting conditions.

The new year of 2002 was off to a grand start for me, whatever the rest of the year might hold.

'Snowdonia's glistening white peaks and the tide-rippled golden sands of Newborough beach…'

Chapter Three

Bodlondeb with Gwilym

My explorations weren't just the trips with Peter, of course. He had his job and his usual activities to keep him busy, and we settled into a routine of getting together a couple of times a week. Sometimes it was just a late walk on the Quay with Gwilym after Camera Club, or an occasional evening out at the North Wales Theatre. On my own for the rest of the time, I often took Gwilym to his favourite places near home.

We follow his nose to the Quay, where two couples sit on a bench, looking at the river while eating takeaway food. Gwil hopes for a handout or some dropped chips, but the defenceless visitors are already besieged by gulls and pigeons, and I drag him away.

A glance toward the castle reveals that the snow is gone from the distant hills above Glan Conwy, on the far side of the

Conwy Valley. After eleven freezing days, this morning is mild again. I miss the snowy views and the bracing cleanness of the colder air, but I'm assured it will return soon. Two couples pose for pictures in front of the six-foot-wide 'Smallest House in Britain', even though it is closed for winter.

The cries of gulls mingle with a loud putt-putting noise from a floating pontoon up near the bridges. (I learn later that the sound is made by the pump used to sluice water over the latest catch of mussels.) Often this walk is musical with clanking and whistling of the wind in the riggings of the many moored boats and the gentle lap of little waves, but today the mildness of the weather is matched by the calmness of the water.

We turn into Bodlondeb (Welsh for contentment), from 1877 to 1937 the estate of Albert Wood. Lawns and small gardens surround the house that is now, with additions, used for Council offices. The native wood still stands on a hill overlooking the estuary and the tarmac Marine Walk provided by Mr. Wood for the people of Conwy.

Now we're in the wood, with robin-song competing with the pump's putt-putt. The wood is small – perhaps covering half of the overall sixty-acre estate – and sits on a headland with views of the estuary on two sides. Paths criss-cross and meander into the woods and out to viewpoints, allowing for longer walks than the wood's size suggests. The trees are mostly pines, firs, and evergreen oaks, with bare birches and beeches on the exposed slope over the river. Holly and shrubs make up the middle tier, and bracken ferns and clumps of green leaves that will produce bluebells in spring cover the ground.

Occasionally, the pleasing clackety-clack of a train floats across the river to us, reminding me of previous trips to Britain and the fact that I am now temporarily living here, not just a typical tourist.

Rounding a bend on the headland, we find the view opens to the Bay and all the way out to the Irish Sea. Gwil leads a zigzag trail into the interior again, to an open glade where blackbirds and squirrels scatter at our intrusion. An open, broken mussel shell lies on the ground, no doubt brought up here by some bird who wanted to eat in peace.

Weaving back to an outside path, we look down on the marina and the gorgeous sight of two oystercatchers taking off and revealing the black and white pattern of their outspread wings. From above, the current is more obvious and shows me the tide is coming in, before I notice that the boats at anchor have turned around. The three-foot stump of a dead tree has become Nature's flower pot, with a circle of bluebells filling its hollow heart. I long to see that in bloom, but I don't think it's possible before I must leave Conwy.

Looking down on the Marine Walk, we see families, bicycles, and dogs. Gwil decides to leave the woods and join this happy band, so we carefully descend the steep, rough path. Rugged and rusty Conwy Mountain looms behind the scene at the water's edge, where shelducks, oystercatchers, and curlews search for food.

I ask an elderly man what the stream is that joins the river here, and he tells me it's from a reservoir on the side of Conwy Mountain, built long ago to pipe water to Llandudno Junction for the steam trains. Noticing his strong accent, I ask if he's a native. Proudly, he tells me he is a Jackdaw, meaning he was born within the circle of Conwy's walls. The black and grey jackdaw, a relative of rooks and crows, is Conwy's logo.

The Marine Walk leads us home, past the spot where, in 1996, Gwil decided that Mona and I should become friends. We don't mind leaving Bodlondeb since we know that we can have another large dose of this "contentment" any time we want.

'Paths criss-cross and meander into the woods and out to viewpoints…' Bodlondeb Wood, Gwilym's favourite place

Chapter Four

Jupiter, High Tides
and a Well Kept Secret

In late January–early February, with three weeks of wind and, at times, gales, the symphony of chandlery was continuous on the Quay. I began to feel that this pleasing clatter, combined with the crying of gulls and shrill piping of oystercatchers would haunt my imagination when I went home – wherever that would be. Since Gwil insisted on the Quay for his last walk before bed, I had the added ambience of the night, which I would certainly never have experienced with any regularity on my own. Views of the floodlit castle with the rays of the full moon dancing on the wind-rippled water created unforgettable images. A heron frequented a certain spot near the bridge at night, and oystercatchers are most vocal in the late evening.

Peter's mate Tony, an astronomy enthusiast, had told us that the bright planet visible in the sky at that time was Jupiter, and I looked for it on clear nights. On the twenty-sixth of January, I took Gwil to the Quay at around six p.m. before leaving him at home alone for the evening. Through a layer of thin clouds, I saw the waxing moon and, very nearby, what I thought must be Jupiter.

Peter picked me up, and we went to his place for dinner. As we walked toward the house, he looked up and said, "I'm sure Jupiter was on the other side of the moon when I got home from work."

My view from the Quay coincided with his, and we didn't know what to make of it. The next day, Tony explained that it had been an Occultation of Jupiter, when the moon passed in front of the planet and hid it from sight temporarily. (Many events we call eclipses are actually occultations; an eclipse is technically only what happens when one body passes into the shadow of another.) We wished we'd known to watch it at the right time, but at least we'd each seen it before and after, and learned something new about the heavens. It added a touch of uniqueness to that one pleasant evening out of many.

Because Gwilym was an unusual dog, people often recognised him and spoke to me. Two men, who spend a lot of time on the river, asked about Mona and introduced themselves when we met with our dogs on the Marine Walk. Returning to the Quay with us, they explained that the half-dozen small open motorboats coming upriver alongside us belonged to the local mussel-men, who were returning from a day's work harvesting the clusters of small shellfish from the riverbed by means of long-handled rakes, in the same way the twelfth-century Cistercian monks, the founders of Aberconwy Abbey, did. After its first rinsing on the pontoon, the catch is taken indoors farther along the Quay, where it is sluiced with fresh water for several days before being shipped to restaurants. Perhaps the strongest interest in them locally is from the gulls and a few crows. Dropped onto the tarmac from on high by the flying birds, the mussel shells break, enabling the birds to extract the flesh. Gwilym liked to go down to the high tide line and look for mussels missed by the gulls, but he crunched them up and ate them, shell and all! I tried to explain to him that the seagulls don't come and steal his food, but it fell on deaf ears.

'The water topped the Quay and ran knee-deep in front of the row of cottages and the pub...' Conwy Quay at high tide on 1 February 2002

Most of the boats bobbing at anchor or pulled up on shore are pleasure craft, with one commercial trawler that fishes for plaice and scallops. Bumping into one of the two men again, I learned about the eight antique wooden fishing boats in the harbour, restored as pleasure boats. His comely prawner was built in 1894.

Our morning walk on 1 February revealed the first crocuses in the churchyard.

It seemed to me there had been more rain in the previous few days than in all the months of my long visit combined. The changes seemed to have brought a pair of great black–backed gulls to the estuary, new birds to me.

Having been told about the exceptionally high tide that was expected, along with high winds, I joined other watchers at one o'clock in the afternoon. The water topped the Quay and ran knee-deep in front of the row of cottages and the pub, where sandbags protected the doorways. Slogging about in waders, the owner of the antique boat said he'd planned to work on it, but hadn't brought his dinghy in far enough and now couldn't reach it. A woman who lives in one of the cottages arrived home and was relieved to find that the men had sandbagged her door, too. The last flood, in 1993, had trapped her inside her cottage for a while. Peter surprised me as I stood watching; he was on his way to work and swung by for a few minutes to check out the high tide. I told him I'd wanted to go on to the Marine Walk but found it flooded, and he told me how, after the water receded, I could extend my usual walk by going on from the end of that tarmac path.

I went home to dry out and wait for the tide to begin falling, then came back out at three p.m. to try this new route. Continuing from the end of the Marine Walk, I went on around the marina and golf course, ending up among sand dunes along the shore near the mouth of the estuary. As the wind whipped the clumps of marram grass in the dunes, the tips of the blades nearest the outside of the tussocks drew arcs in the sand, as if with a compass. It was a cheery detail I'd never noticed anywhere before.

Nearby, I read a plaque commemorating the work of local engineers in 1944. It said that one of the best kept secrets of WWII was the work done here in building concrete sections of Mulberry Harbour, a complex floating harbour installation, essential to the success of landing troops and supplies on D-Day. The prototype units were designed in Bangor, and the sections of harbour were constructed at this site and launched into the

Conwy River. Secrecy was vital throughout, and even the hundreds of men employed on the project were unaware of the purpose of their work. Conwy can be justly proud of pulling off all aspects of the operation and playing a significant role in winning the war.

Across the estuary, Deganwy overlooks the Bay, which was choppy with whitecaps whipped up by the freshening wind. Perching beneath its namesake 'mountain' – resembling a slightly askew sandwich cake – Deganwy is an attractive Victorian resort but has never been much more than a small village. It once had a busy little harbour, shipping out slate from quarries up in the Conwy valley, but the old sailing ships have long since gone. Having read of Deganwy's historic role in guarding the north shore of the entry to Conwy, I hoped one day to explore the scant ruins of the castle that often figured in the area's history until Llewelyn the Last destroyed it in 1263.

Behind me stretched the colourful, sheep-dotted contours of Conwy Mountain, and the 360-degree views were very pleasing. "What a place!" I thought and remembered warnings I'd been given about *hiraeth*, the longing for Wales that grips those who leave.

Chapter Five

St. Dwynwen Meets St. Valentine

Americans do not generally have the same reserve that the British have cultivated, and it became obvious to Peter early on that I was smitten. But since he didn't have the same reaction, he didn't know quite what to do with the fact that we were so compatible and comfortable together. Somehow – the memory is lost in all the conversations and emotions that followed – we began to talk about the possibility that we could be more than just friends.

It wasn't just that he was a fifty-something bachelor, unsure of whether he could adjust to sharing his space and his life; this typical reaction of unmarried men was complicated by the fact that he and his brother had built Peter's house themselves. If you have decided every detail of your house and lifestyle on your own, how easy is it to invite someone else to move in and make it her home as well? And moving to a new home we'd choose together would not be an option. He worried that it wouldn't be fair to me to ask me to move into a home with everything already well established, while all I wanted was to be with him in that house in Wales.

Discussions always came back to the conclusion that being good friends was the only thing that made sense. But lurking beneath that idea was the painful bottom-line, that if Peter wanted to be with me as much as I wanted to be with him, we wouldn't be talking about the practical issues of a possible future together.

On Valentine's Day, Peter again showed his natural

romantic streak, but I was soon to look back on our trip to Llanddwyn Island on Anglesey as our last really good time together.

Returning to Newborough, to the beach where we'd strolled with Tony and Gretta on New Year's Day, we walked in the opposite direction, to a Nature Conservancy Reserve. Along that morning's tide line we saw a jelly fish, small crab, a cuttlefish bone, several Mermaid's purses (egg case of the lesser spotted dogfish), and many empty egg cases of the common whelk, which reminded me of brains. The variety of shells and colourful stones – especially green and deep purple – was much greater than at Conwy. Cormorants were doing Dracula impersonations, gulls and oystercatchers perched on the rocks, basking in the sun. Well back from the water, the edge of the forest of Corsican pines that had been planted to stabilise the sand had apparently been damaged in the recent high tides. A vertical face about fifteen feet high had been cut in the dunes, and a row of uprooted pines littered the boundary of forest and beach.

After crossing the causeway that is submerged during the highest tides, we left the beach behind and headed over grassy, heathery, bracken-clad hillocks, where frequent outcrops of rocks host a wide variety of lichens and mosses.

Named after St. Dwynwen, the Welsh patron saint of romance, Llanddwyn Island is another place where natural beauty and human history combine to make something really special. St. Dwynwen's Day is the twenty-fifth of January, and Valentine's Day is less important in Wales than elsewhere, but we made it a cross-cultural theme by celebrating the Welsh saint on Valentine's Day.

In the fifth century, Dwynwen was in love with a man her father thought not good enough, and he refused to give him her hand. (I have read three different versions of why she didn't marry him, and this is the one I prefer. Who knows

'An old light on the point of the island proved to be too low and the lighthouse was added in 1845.' One of many sheltered beaches on Llanddwyn Island

what really happened?) She prayed to be cured of her love and never to fall in love again. Dwynwen took the veil and later became a saint, and every faithful lover who invoked her help was either relieved of the passion, or obtained the object of his or her affection. The island and a well that was used for predicting the future of lovers became places of pilgrimage. A plain Latin cross in her honour was erected near the lighthouse in modern times. The ruins of a Medieval Benedictine abbey stand nearby.

A picnic lunch in sunshine followed our walk, and, to my surprise, Peter produced "the last two mince pies from the freezer" for dessert, along with a flask of peppermint tea, which he knew I preferred. It was another of those bittersweet

Jake greeted me each morning at the Town House B & B

moments that could have been really special if we had shared the same feelings.

The views from our picnic spot included the lighthouse, historic pilot houses, the rocky shore, the mountains of the Lleyn Peninsula, and the Snowdon range across the Menai Straits, with new snow on the two highest peaks. An old light on the point of Llanddwyn had proved to be too low, and the lighthouse was added in 1845. In front of the picturesque row of pilot houses sits a cannon, which was used for signalling the village of Newborough in case of a ship in distress. A lifeboat house and, nearby, a Celtic cross in memory of all who died, are reminders of the dangers in these treacherous waters.

With cursory looks at the historic sites and hopes of returning with more time on another day, we hurried back over the hillocks, looking down on numerous small, sheltered beaches set among natural rock enclosures.

Our hurrying was because we were going to meet Mona,

who was due back from the U.S. Gwilym was very happy to have his Mum back and seemed to like having both of us fussing over him.

But to avoid being in the way, after a few days I moved to the Town House, a B&B on Rose Hill Street, where I befriended another elderly dog and enjoyed getting to know the proprietors, Alan and Elaine. Jake, a Welsh sheep dog, had had three homes in his first eight months and, having been badly treated, had developed a habit of biting people. Alan and Elaine rescued him when they lived in the country, and he quickly responded to their loving care by becoming very sweet-tempered. After their move to the B&B, he became a favourite with many guests. Jake maintained a puppyish playfulness, in spite of painful arthritis, and it was a delight to meet him at the bottom of the stairs each morning, with a toy in his mouth, hoping for a game before breakfast.

Peter seemed more distant after Valentine's Day, and I felt that his plans for my birthday a fortnight later were only made so that I wouldn't be disappointed. Our trip to Llyn Crafnant above Trefriw was our final outing. Crafnant nestles below very attractive high hills that stand between the Conwy Valley and Snowdon. From the road we had glimpses of the high peaks, well covered with snow once again. Our walk around the lake included views of historic mines high up on the steep hillsides – one slate and the other lead. Cascading streams and brief snow flurries added to the atmosphere, and we took a tea break beside a musical, little, multi-level waterfall. Because it was my birthday, rather than our usual picnic, we had lunch at the Tannery in Llanrwst.

I knew these two days would be major contributors to the hiraeth that lay in store for me. Would I, I wondered, be able to distinguish between hiraeth and losing Peter? At the same time, I was becoming familiar with a traditional Welsh song that was on a tape I'd bought to take home with me. Written by Joseph Parry, first professor of music at Aberystwyth University in the late 1800s, 'Myfanwy' tells the story of the professor's rejection by his childhood sweetheart. In the last verse, he wishes her 'a lifetime beneath the midday sunshine's glow' and asks for her hand in a final farewell. It's a sad, pretty tune, and I knew it would echo in my mind long after I left Wales. I felt an affinity with the Professor and wondered if he had ever gone to Llanddwyn Island, to invoke the saint's help in curing him of his unrequited love.

'We had lunch in Llanrwst...' The tower of the church of St. Grwst seen from the adjoining historic Gwydir chapel

Chapter Six

The Wave Nobody Saw

After all the wonderful times we'd shared, how I dreaded parting. Peter must have been dreading it in his own way, too, probably worrying about how I'd handle it. So he pulled back a fortnight before I was to leave Conwy. What a blow that was! I thought we'd settled on staying friends, and I didn't understand why we couldn't go on as we were until I had to leave, but he had become too uncomfortable with the situation.

I considered moving on earlier than planned. The last days of my trip were to be spent in Dumfries, Scotland, where I'd be attending a meeting before flying home from Glasgow. But I shouldn't have liked staying alone that long in the hotel where the meeting would be held, so I'd have had to find a B&B and move twice. It was easier just to stay in my cosy, familiar room on Rose Hill Street, where the quiet understanding of Alan and Elaine was such a comfort.

Having done some volunteer work for the RSPB throughout my stay, I began working five days a week to fill my days, which was also a big help. But that left two lonely weekends, and the memories of Chester, on a bright day, when I seemed to be the only person on my own in that interesting and busy city, and of the brilliant fields of daffodils at Bodnant Garden are just a painful blur.

Peter and I met once more, at Camera Club, and said goodbye afterwards, with a quick hug beside his car in the Station car park. I wanted to keep it brief to avoid crying, and

'Memories of the brilliant fields of daffodils...'
Bodnant Gardens in March

settled on one word: "*Diolch.*" I'd learned a few Welsh words during my stay and hoped that saying thank you in Welsh would give it more meaning, since I couldn't take a chance on a whole sentence of specific thanks in English.

Assuming that he was relieved to have me gone from Conwy, I would have been very surprised to read what he wrote soon after I left. The day that I took the train from the Junction, he climbed Tal-y-Fan, the closest of the Snowdonia peaks to his home, and sat gazing at the scene before him, watching for my train.

> ... He (writing of himself in the third person) had recently said goodbye to a very dear friend and, not knowing if or when they might meet again, much of the joy seemed to have drained from his spirit. ... At about eleven o'clock he watched a train pulling out of Llandudno Junction Station

and followed it as it slowly snaked its way through Mochdre and on towards Colwyn Bay. He could but wonder as to the various destinations of the passengers: to Chester and then maybe south towards London, or north to Scotland and even further afield.

As it disappeared into the hazy distance he raised his arm and waved; a wave that no one would ever see – not even the sheep that silently grazed on the hillside nearby.

Blaming myself for having ruined what could have been a meaningful friendship and for ending my six-month adventure as unsettled as when I'd started, I flew to the States with the certainty that I would never see or hear from Peter again.

The months away from home and the disappointment at the end had distilled one thing in my mind, however: I would go back to Lancaster County, Pennsylvania, where I'd grown up and where three of my siblings and their families would be nearby. With most of my adult life having been spent in California, I wasn't sure if 'P.A.' would still feel like home to me, but it seemed like the best idea. At least it was a lot closer to Britain in case I decided to resume the sort of wandering there that I'd done during my holidays from 1988 until I met Peter.

Welsh immigrants had played a big part in the settlement of the colony of Pennsylvania, and Quakers seeking religious freedom made up one-third of the population by 1700. In the 1800s, a new wave of Welsh immigration brought steel workers, coal miners, and slate quarrymen. Throughout the US, people of Welsh ancestry have always been a small group; they are more plentiful in Pennsylvania than in any other state.

But that is not my heritage. My great-great-great-great-great-great-grandfather, Christian Wenger, left Switzerland and sailed for America in 1727 on what historians call the

'*Mennonite Mayflower*.' My father grew up in an Old Order Mennonite home, and didn't learn to speak English until he went to the local one-roomed schoolhouse. (Such picturesque structures are still in common use in rural areas of Lancaster County.) My father left home at sixteen and changed his lifestyle, but many of my relatives follow the old ways, travelling by horse and buggy, using no electricity, and speaking the German dialect commonly known as 'Pennsylvania Dutch' as much as possible.

Moving back among these peace-loving people was deeply satisfying, and I loved driving the back roads and admiring their tidy farms and gardens and handsome horses. I treasure the childhood memories of visits to my uncles' farms and the gentle evenings in their lantern-lit homes. As the women sat together and talked of family matters in English (for my mother's sake), I liked to creep towards the men's corner and listen to the soft cadences of their conversation, even though I couldn't understand the language. Perhaps my natural sympathy with efforts to preserve the Welsh language comes from growing up among my father's people.

A year's lease on a flat in an old, converted, semi-detached house in my hometown of Ephrata, a good used car, some furniture, and my boxes from California: my new life was underway. There was enough excitement and discovery to keep me occupied and cheerful. I loved my independence and began volunteering at a place of fond earlier memories, a living-history farm called Landis Valley Museum, where I soon learned the names of all the work horses, the cows, and the young ox-in-training. Making new friends there and at church, I also enjoyed renewing old friendships and seeing a lot of my sister and her family.

One month after leaving Conwy, determined to forget Peter as quickly as possible, I received his first letter. I had given him my sister's address while I was still seeing him frequently and had invited him to write. One month after his first letter came his first phone call. It wasn't over after all, but now what?

We exchanged letters and photos, and I enjoyed telling him about my hometown and new life. I wanted him to see that I was doing okay on my own. He shared my photos with friends at Camera Club, and I received e-mails from a friend in the club, saying how pretty the rolling hills of Pennsylvania Dutch farm country appeared and how pleased Peter was to hear from me.

One of my letters that summer included photos of a waterfowl area that had been created after I'd moved to California. I loved this new place, Middle Creek Wildlife Management Area, twelve miles from my flat, and spent a lot of time there, often taking some of my sister's grandchildren. On the back of a photo of Sunfish Pond I wrote, "Wouldn't you like to see that hillside of deciduous trees in autumn colour?" I felt it was safer than coming right out and inviting him in the letter.

During our next phone conversation, trying to sound casual, I said, "So, do you want to come and see the autumn colours?"

His reply, "I would, actually," nearly floored me. Much indecision followed as he worried that coming to see me would seem more of a commitment than he intended. On the phone, I kept saying, "It's only a trip, Peter; just enjoy it."

As the time approached for his visit, my sister Joyce kept saying to me, "You're just a tour guide; you're just a tour guide."

His trip went smoothly and we had delightful drives and walks around the area, even though it was a bit early for the peak of autumn colour. Revealing that I'd been trying to learn his National Anthem from a tape, I asked him to sing it with me as we drove down a country road somewhere in Pennsylvania.

A major event was the brief visit of Mary Ellen, a dear friend from California, who flew in for a quick visit to meet Peter and to see me in my new place. They liked each other, as I knew they would.

Near the end of the fortnight, we talked again, and concluded we were just friends. I was prepared this time and not terribly upset. But I couldn't resist saying to him, "Oh, you foolish man! It could have been so good!"

A change was taking place, however. He'd seen me in a different light – emotionally stable and capable of making a life for myself, a competent and confident driver and route-planner, settled and content on my own. I sensed his growing admiration. Through all the months he'd been keeping me at arm's length, he was still the man who couldn't resist the urge to push a Christmas card through my letterbox early on the morning after we met.

Back in Conwy, he continued to ring me, and, after a fortnight, he surprised me by saying, "I miss you." He seemed to be lingering when I felt the conversation was finished, and then, to my further amazement, he said he'd been thinking about "possibilities."

My romantic response? "Oh, Peter! How can you do this to me?"

The state of 'Friendship-with-possibilities' continued over the winter and led to my booking a ticket to fly to Manchester in mid-March for a two-month visit. I e-mailed Alan and Elaine at my old B&B to ask if they were willing to have me for another long stay. Graciously, they said yes.

Three days before my trip, I returned to Middle Creek. The snow geese were passing through on their way to Canada, and I'd gone several times that week, trying to get my fill of the amazing spectacle. At the peak of the migration, there can be 120,000 snow geese at this site. This last trip was at dusk, on the advice of the man in the visitor centre. On the eleventh of March, wave after wave of snow geese, Canada geese, and swans flew in overhead at Willow Point, coming together for overnight safety on the lake. It was breath-taking and awe-inspiring. Would I ever want to leave this permanently? But I knew Britain offers some of the outstanding bird-watching experiences in the world, and how I should love seeing more of them with Peter.

'We exchanged letters and photos…' Peter's photo of heather on Conwy mountain rekindled my desire to see North Wales in other seasons

Chapter Seven

With Ambience to Spare

Peter met me at Manchester airport, on the first day of his week's holiday, and as we crossed the border into Wales, he turned on a tape that he had previously set to play 'We'll keep a welcome in the hillsides.' The question that came to my mind had to remain unspoken: what about the line, 'We'll kiss away each hour of hiraeth?'

We packed a lot of scenic trips into his week off – some familiar and some new to me. Throughout my two-month visit, we also took advantage of his working mostly evening shifts by doing half-day jaunts close to home, with his two rest days each week adding to our available trip time.

Revisiting the gorgeous daffodils at Bodnant Garden, but this time happily and with Peter; watching the tumbling flight of lapwings and identifying numerous birds at RSPB Conwy; picnicking in Betws-y-Coed, and walking along the River Lledr in warm sunshine were pure pleasure.

One of Peter's favourite spots since childhood is Parc Mawr, where the wood opens out into hilly sheep pastures and climbs gradually to high rolling moors. The ruined and roofless stone farmhouses standing in this remote, stark landscape were probably summer homes years ago, when whole families relocated with their animals to higher pastures for the warmer months.

On the cliff-topped moors we saw several choughs, after Peter recognised the call and focused the binoculars on them.

What a thrill was this, my first sighting of one of Britain's rare birds, their red-orange beaks and legs vivid against their glossy black bodies. Most of the one thousand pairs in the British Isles are in Ireland, but it is only in Wales that they will also breed on an inland rock-face as well as their usual coastal cliffs.

From the first, I had taken to moors, as I had the deserts of Southern California and the barren rocky reaches above timberline in the High Sierra. I've always been grateful that I was given a disposition that sees beauty even where there are no brilliant colours or lush views. The wide lonesomeness of moors appeals to my romantic streak, and the complete newness of them for an American makes them fascinating. This small taste of moorland in Wales made me want to see a broader expanse, as I had a few times in Scotland.

Medieval Llangelynin Old Church sits, at 927 feet, near the top of the hills, surrounded by its walled churchyard. It was built of stone on a sixth-century foundation, with a slate roof, a little enclosed stone porch, a thick wooden door with wrought iron fixtures, and a stone bell-cote open on two sides in the Welsh style. Inside, there are faded texts written on the walls, also a very old Welsh custom. Occasionally, the curved wooden beams still ring with music, when services are held there on the third Sunday afternoon of each month in summer.

From the other side of the hills, the church is accessible by narrow country roads, and these became our homeward path. A new church was built lower down the valley in the eighteenth century, and I found Peter's memory of being taken there for Harvest Festivals charming. Along with other pupils from Ysgol Llangelynin in Henryd, he peered up at the minister's face, framed by the corn sheaves that decorated the pulpit. The deconsecrated 'new' church is now a sculptor's studio.

Cwm Idwal on a glorious day in March will always stand out in my memory. That glaciated, rocky bowl, towered over by the rough precipices of Glyder Fawr and the Devil's Kitchen, is sublime. We lingered long in the sunshine over our picnic on a large flat rock, and finished our walk around the wild, natural lake as the sinking sun gilded the rocks, which, in turn, cast golden reflections in the lake. The legend of Llyn Idwal makes it sound a spooky place, claiming that no bird will fly across the dark water of the lake where Prince Idwal was murdered by his foster brother nine hundred years ago. But there was none of that mood as we revelled in the alpine feeling on a bright winter day.

The short path to Swallow Falls is *de rigueur* for all visitors to Betws-y-Coed, but Peter took me to the viewpoint on the opposite bank. Leaving the car on the side of a minor road, we walked along a forestry track, then down a steep footpath that turns and contours along the side of a cliff high above the riverside. One section of this trail is backed by a high, lichen-covered, granite face that loomed above us, but gentler forested scenes follow when the rock outcrop ends. After the larches of the Forestry Commission, native broadleaves take over. A fence makes this narrow path safe, although "Perygl" signs warn of the dangers of old lead mines, presumably somewhere below the fence where no reasonable person would ever venture.

All the while, the roar of falling and cascading water increased, drawing us on to a fine viewpoint framed by oak and birch trees. Here a bench is provided where the desire to linger is strongest. The upper falls are fractured by rugged rocks into diverse smaller channels that rejoin in a rather eerie, deep, dark pool. Continuing its charge, the water exits the pool by means of a narrow funnel in the rocks, from which it spills out in a wide, lace curtain. The River Llugwy goes on cascading and tumbling over rocks on its way to an eventual meeting with the Conwy.

The footpath continues on up above the falls and offers delightful scenes of plants growing among tilted, striated rocks, and a sideways cascade around a rocky island. We sat here for a while, too, watching the antics of a tree creeper.

The temptation to stop in Betws for an ice cream was quashed by Peter's need to get home and prepare for work, but the beauty we'd walked with that morning lived on through more mundane activities.

There is more to the seemingly deserted village of Aberffraw on the west coast of Anglesey than meets the eye. The area's layered history boasts a Mesolithic camp from around 7,000 B.C., followed by Bronze Age settlements. In its greatest glory, Aberffraw was the seat of the House of Gwynedd, which provided Welsh princes for nearly 1,000 years, and in more modern times, it was an important port and commercial centre.

Having stopped to photograph the appealing arched bridge, we walked through the quiet village and along a riverside path that overlooks the tidal River Ffraw and the dunes of Tywyn Aberffraw Nature Reserve. Two large kites were being flown on the sands below us, and we marvelled at the strength needed to control them in such a wind. Ubiquitous yellow gorse complemented the deep blue of the river and the turquoise water of Aberffraw Bay, backed by the distant mountains of Snowdonia and the Lleyn Peninsula.

Continuing around to the coast, we came to St. Cwyfan-in-the-Sea, a charming little church that was founded in the early seventh century, rebuilt in the twelfth, and restored in the nineteenth. Situated on a tiny island, the church was threatened by centuries of erosion and was stabilised in the nineteenth century by an encircling wall. The building and roof were in a ruinous state until parts of the structure were demolished and the roof was repaired over what remained. Having climbed the steps in the wall, we found a setting of grass and pink sea thrift. The church cannot be reached during high tide, and waves crash over the roof during storms. We not only got there at the right time for the tide, but while we were on the island, a couple came to inspect the interior, with an eye to getting it ready for occasional summer use. Except for lots of dust, it was in good shape. Seeing the interior of the little stone church that seats sixty people was a real treat, and we learned that the exposed beams are the originals, dating from the seventh century. From the lime-washed walls and plain glass windows to the wooden chairs, altar table, and pulpit, simplicity was the rule. There are just the two side aisles, and the chairs are arranged five across. The seaward wall has no windows; from the outside we saw that the bell is missing from the bell-cote.

Viewing it from a nearby hill, with dark rocks and yellow gorse in the foreground, we also wished to see it in more dramatic circumstances – high tide and rough seas. Perhaps another time; but for a first visit, ours had been perfect.

Our walk on a cloudy Sunday afternoon from the Green Gorge above Penmaenmawr to a group of Bronze Age standing stones known as Druid's Circle was rich with atmosphere. The map reveals many other prehistoric sites in this area awaiting our exploration in the future, but I doubt any will have the impact this place had for me. Lying beyond the old Craiglwyd granite quarry and the site of an ancient stone axe factory, Druid's Circle is surrounded by green hills that lead the eye to the rougher hills of Conwy Mountain, Penmaen-Bach, Foel Lus, and on to the sea and the Great Orme. Waving gracefully in the breeze, long golden grasses softened the hard contours of the standing stones. Hill ponies and sheep, meandering and munching, added to the scene, and when a white pony stood silhouetted on the skyline above the stone circle, the mood was truly ancient and quintessentially British.

'Occasionally the curved wooden beams still ring with music...'
Honey overlooking Llangelynin Old Church

Chapter Eight

Generating Power, Defending Power

Knowing Peter had to be back for work at four p.m., we packed our lunch and headed for the pass called Nant Gwynant. The 1958 Snowdonia National Park Guide says of the valley's two lakes:

> Their shape and setting among native woodlands and great rock masses of singular beauty give this pass a claim to first rank in natural scenery.

First stop: an overlook with views of Llyn Gwynant nestled below a line of peaks. Mount Snowdon is directly across from the viewpoint. Sheep grazed the very green valley floor, the lake reflected the blue sky, and the varied greys and browns of the peaks added drama to this most appealing scene. At the base of the steep, bracken-covered hillside across the valley, we could see the quaint, little, stone-built Cwm Dyli power station, and the pipeline that brings its water supply from Llyn Llydaw. Affectionately known locally as 'the chapel in the valley,' it must be the smallest hydroelectric station in Wales. As we prepared to drive away, a male chaffinch hopped onto the outside mirror of the car, begging for a hand-out.

Opposite: 'Llyn Dinas was as far as we could go that day...'
The lower of the two scenic lakes in Nant Gwynant

Driving down to Llyn Gwynant, we enjoyed the addition of another colour to the palette as the yellow of gorse complemented the sparkling, wind-rippled lake. Llyn Dinas was as far as we could go that day, and we strolled along the shore and ate our lunch before returning home.

Nant Gwynant and Llanberis Pass form two sides of a triangle around Mt. Snowdon, and it was interesting to see them only three days apart. The second trip had no time constraints, which was good because there was so much to see. Having never been over Llanberis Pass before, I was quite taken with its rugged beauty. We wandered around the stream near Pont Cromlech, watching rock climbers on the crags high above, and admiring the colours in the rocks and the dramatic views in all directions. We had a brighter day than H.V. Morton, who described the pass in romantic terms:

> The dark hills narrow on either side. A thin rain is falling. The water shines on the rocks. There is no sound but the plaintive bleating of mountain sheep and the rush of streams falling from the hills. This is the Pass of Llanberis. ... High up the hill-side great rocks are poised as if they had been left there from some old battle of giants.... The memories that live up in the black Valhalla of the Welsh hills are memories strange to the English mind. They are of kings who were half poets, and poets who were half kings; of queer things that happened in the dark, and in the half light; ...

Our main objective was Dinorwig Power Station, a massive hydroelectric plant hidden inside a mountain, and a striking contrast to 'the chapel in the valley' on the other side of the ridge. I was lucky to see Dinorwig with Peter, who worked on the construction of the tunnels for eight years, on his second civil engineering job following university.

Very near the Welsh Slate Museum at Llanberis and immediately adjacent to Snowdonia National Park, the plant utilized and extended two-hundred-year-old quarrying excavations, to avoid further destruction of the environment. The result, built in the 1970s, is the longest man-made tunnel network in Europe, housing the largest pumped storage power plant in the UK. Two existing lakes are used, and water travels through a one-mile tunnel before falling fourteen hundred feet down a thirty-foot diameter shaft, from the higher lake to the lower reservoir. When electricity rates are lowest at night, the water is pumped back up to the higher lake. Unlike most power plants, Dinorwig's six turbines can produce electricity in twelve seconds from start-up.

Along with other environmental concerns, a diversion tunnel was built around the lower lake to allow salmon and sea trout to continue their annual migrations, and rare Arctic char from Llyn Peris were relocated to nearby lakes.

Three submerged boats were found at different times during construction, and two are on display in the visitor centre. The design and the layered, gnarly oak strips of the twenty-foot Elizabethan Peris boat made it ruggedly handsome. Dating from the late 1500s, it is a typical boat of North Wales at that time, the building method having come from earlier Viking invaders.

Overlooking Llyn Peris since the early thirteenth-century, Dolbadarn Castle is a truly Welsh castle, and we scrambled around its ruined tower, forty feet in diameter, with eight-foot thick walls. The large, famous castles of Wales, including Conwy, were built by the English King Edward I as part of a plan for an 'iron ring of castles' to subdue the rebellious Welsh, who were strongly opposed to English occupation. Both the English and the Welsh castles were built of locally quarried materials: slate blocks and rubble mortar at Dolbadarn and, at Conwy, blocks of Silurian grit formed by fine sediments of clay.

Edward's sites appear to have been better chosen for long-term use, however, as all nine of his Welsh castle towns are still flourishing. The Welsh ruins of Dolbadarn, Dolwyddelan, and Bere stand forsaken on their remote hilltops.

Dolbadarn was built before 1230 by Llewelyn the Great, prince of this area of Wales from 1200 to 1240, and the most powerful ruler in Medieval Wales. (A statue of him is the focal point of Lancaster Square in Conwy.) From 1255 to 1275, Dolbadarn was the prison of Owain Goch, who was defeated by his younger brother, Llewelyn the Last (grandsons of Llewelyn the Great).

After the death of Llewelyn the Last, Edward I annexed Wales in 1282, and Dolbadarn Castle was seized by the English; the building of Conwy Castle followed in 1283-87.

The next English king, Edward II, was born in Caernarfon and declared by his father, in 1301, to be the Prince of Wales.

An interesting connection, however, came through Owen Tudor, eighth generation down from Llewelyn the Great. Owen Tudor, the "Rose of Anglesey," handsome and an accomplished dancer, was noticed by Queen Catherine at a ball, after the death in 1422 of the English King Henry V. The widowed queen married the handsome Welshman, and their grandson became Henry VII, founder of the Tudor dynasty of English monarchs, which lasted one hundred and eighteen years. Once again, Welsh blood ran strong in the veins of the next two Princes of Wales.

Chapter Nine

On Top of the Down

Having seen only Cardiff and Brecon during a previous trip, I was thrilled with the prospect of seeing more of South Wales with Peter. When I asked him to attend the John Buchan Society AGM and dinner with me in Chipping Norton in the spring of 2003, he suggested a driving tour that would include his old stamping grounds from Swansea University days. The opportunity to gain further insights into his life was almost as intriguing as the trip itself.

Peter knew very little of the Scottish author, John Buchan, and during our travels I was able to point out several Buchan connections with Wales: family holidays in the Brecon Beacons from 1929 to 1933, fishing in mid-Wales, and a rest cure at Ruthin Castle in North Wales in 1938.

Palm Sunday afternoon found us saying goodbye to my friends in 'Chippy' and heading for South Wales, where we met Peter's cousin Pam. Pleased by her desire to meet me, even though there was still nothing definite between Peter and me, I was prey to all the usual feelings of wanting to make a good impression. We got on well together, and she immediately put me at my ease. She came to pick us up at our B&B the next morning, and took us for a scenic drive through the Wye valley. Expansive, rolling, green hills plunged down to the river far below, its banks lined with the white flowers of blackthorn. Hillsides echoed that look, with white flowering wild cherry scattered among the many bright greens of new leaves and buds on native trees.

We said our farewells over lunch before continuing on our journey towards Swansea. In beautiful sunshine, we headed west from Monmouth through Abergavenny and over the Heads of the Valleys road as far as Hirwaun. Climbing over the Rhigos Mountain, we admired the view back down towards the Vale of Glyn-Neath, while farther to the north we could see the distant outline of Black Mountain and the Brecon Beacons. It was such a lovely day and never has ice cream tasted better than those we purchased from the van in the summit car park. We could have lingered in this tranquil, remote place but it was mid-afternoon and we still had a long way to go. We carried on downhill, into that best known of all the South Wales valleys – Cwm Rhondda – down through the winding streets of Treherbert and Treorchy.

Seeing this well known coal mining area for the first time, with its rows of terraced houses where miners lived, evoked images from *How Green Was My Valley* and H.V. Morton's visit to Rhondda. In 1932 he wrote:

> If the thousands of people who go gaily through the mountain passes of Snowdonia and haunt the ruins of dead castles would spend only a few days in the South, talking to the people, trying to understand their situation, attempting to visualise the hard facts of their lives, the nation might in time bring a little more sympathy and understanding to the problems of the Welsh coal-field.

Climbing westward over the mountains towards Port Talbot, through several isolated hamlets, we eventually caught our first glimpse of Swansea Bay. During our quick drive around Swansea, Peter remarked on how much the city has changed since his university days. Pointing out the new shopping centre, he also explained that part of the old docks has been transformed into a marina, and what used to be semi-derelict land on the east side of the city is now a retail park.

Clyne Castle was an unlikely hall of residence, but that is where Peter spent three years while studying Civil Engineering in the early 1970s. Overlooking Swansea Bay, about halfway between Swansea and Oystermouth, Clyne Castle was originally a private residence, built in 1791. The castellated house was renamed Clyne Castle in 1860 by the new owner, a copper millionaire who greatly improved the gardens. Clyne Gardens, with their spectacular springtime displays of azaleas and rhododendrons, are now owned and maintained by Swansea City Council. Three familiar trees caught my eye: two unusually large Monterey cypresses, growing better here than on their native windswept coastline in California, and one Giant Sequoia. Peter said that he had passed those trees countless times and never dreamed that he'd one day have a close friend to whom the Sequoia would be so very familiar. In late afternoon, as we headed out towards Gower, the sun illuminated the white lighthouse and islands of the Mumbles.

Lovely bays, sandy beaches and dunes, rugged limestone cliffs, the ruins of a 12th-century Norman castle, hill ponies, long, rectangular fields that follow medieval patterns, and unforgettable views – where else but the famous Gower Peninsula? We walked in warm sunshine from Southgate to Three Cliffs Bay along gorse-covered cliff tops, and down to the wide beach flanked by the jagged three cliffs. Turning inland, we waded through the shallow, sparkling Pennard Pill, flowing from Cwm Ilston, and climbed a steep path through high dunes, to see the ruins of Pennard Castle. This outpost of Henry I was built in an attempt to subdue the Welsh natives, just as his great-great-great-grandson, Edward I, would do in Conwy, some 150 years later. As we returned to the beach, a young woman on horseback, with a dog running alongside, splashed through the stream, the silhouetted cliffs forming a striking backdrop to the enchanting scene.

Port Eynon, with its attractive old church, handsome lifeboat memorial and dune-backed beach, was our next stop as we made our way west to Rhosili Bay. Climbing through gorse and heather to the highest point on Gower, we sat in the sun atop Rhosili Down, talking and enjoying the views, for a long time. A swallow, newly returned from wintering in Africa, kept us company.

Dominating our view was Worms Head, two strangely eroded rocky islets, stretching a mile into the Bay and rising 200 feet above the water. In the sand between us and this 'sea serpent,' the bare ribs of the *Helvetia*, a Norwegian ship that was wrecked here during a storm in 1887, protruded, visible only at low tide.

The coastline to the north stretches out towards the island of Burry Holms and Burry Inlet, which separates North Gower from the mainland of South Wales. At our back, on the high ground behind Rhosili Down, lay a patchwork of fields – reminding us of Gower's dual economy of tourism and farming.

In this setting of flowers, flitting birds, and lovely views, we had our first significant talk about the future, although we didn't make any definite plans. With such encouraging words, and in such a place, how could it not be my favourite part of the whole trip?

A cream tea, enjoyed while overlooking the Bay, was followed by a walk around the cliff tops that lead to Worms Head, but the tide was coming in by then and it was too late to venture onto the rocks. Again we sat and absorbed it all as the sun sank lower. Lambs sought their dams as we strolled among numerous hill ponies to Worms Head Pub for a fish dinner *alfresco*. Denied a colourful sunset by a bank of fog over the water, we were treated instead to a spectacular full moon, huge and golden, as it broke free from the horizon. Driving

'We sat in the sun atop Rhosili Down, enjoying the views...'
Worm's Head from Rhosili Down

back to our rooms in Southgate, we enjoyed the surrounding countryside bathed in its mystical, silvery light.

As H. V. Morton put it:

> I shall always think of Gower as a place where herds of wild-looking ponies stand among golden gorse, and where the sea whispers by day and night to little lonely bays.

We left that lovely peninsula the next morning to drive the length of Wales, back to Conwy.

A nearly road-less area on the map of South Wales had intrigued me for years: a river runs north-south, the only east-west road is designated as Scenic, and the words 'Cambrian

Mountains' stretch across the mottled background. I asked Peter if we might follow the river north from Llandovery and take that Scenic Road to Tregaron, and he readily agreed.

The mountains here are not as high as Snowdonia, but this area is possibly the most remote in Wales. The building of access roads for hikers, climbers and tourists in Snowdonia has made the difference between the northern and southern areas. Beyond Llandovery, our route followed narrow country lanes. Silver birches and a variety of little wildflowers bedecked the verge, and recent roadside work revealed the ancient art of hedge layering. Later on, we stopped again to peer down into a steep-sided valley where the sparkling blue Tywi had cut its way through the rough terrain eons ago. Very rugged, rocky outcrops mix with the soft green of the steep hillsides, and native ash, alder, hazel and oak create a pleasant atmosphere in the area where the Tywi was dammed in 1972 to provide an additional water supply for Swansea.

While sitting near Llyn Brianne, we watched a lone bird gliding gracefully over the lake. As it turned and soared upwards we recognised it by the unmistakable shape of its forked tail. It was a red kite, the first I'd ever seen! While we ate our lunch, this majestic bird gave us a prolonged look at its beautiful markings – a reddish body with white patches on its black-tipped wings. Having heard of the threats to the red kite's safety and its comeback in Britain added to the deep satisfaction of seeing one at last.

As we climbed higher, the green hills were replaced by high moors of golden grasses, gorse and heather. We saw little evidence of human activities, other than forestry work, until we reached Tregaron.

Cors Tregaron Nature Reserve is three square miles of peat bogs, and we hoped, when passing it, to see more red kites in one of their best known habitats. But we only saw one, farther along the road, when it swooped close to the car, giving us another good look. The stirring sightings of red kites became one of the lasting treasures of this marvellous trip.

After the tranquillity of Tregaron Bog, the streets of Aberystwyth seemed crowded and busy. Ready for a break from driving, we strolled along the seafront, enjoying a refreshing breeze off the sea. We looked at the university buildings with added interest, knowing that the grandson of Peter's cousin Dina would soon be studying there.

Renewed and refreshed, we set off on the last leg of our journey home. North of Machynlleth, the surrounding scenery was noticeably more rugged, and when we saw the southern flanks of Cader Idris with the shining waters of Tal-y-Llyn nestling in the valley below, we felt we were surely getting into North Wales.

On through Dolgellau and Trawsfynydd, we were soon surrounded by the slate tips of Blaenau Ffestiniog.

As we reached the top of the Crimea Pass, we gazed on the classic profile of Moel Siabod with the top of its southern slopes just catching the last rays of the setting sun. This was a mountain I had come to know quite well, as Peter had pointed it out from numerous viewpoints. Here it was again, seemingly welcoming us home.

The light was fading as we drove down through Dolwyddelan and into the shadows of the Lledr Valley. Another half-hour and we were safely in Conwy, reflecting on a truly delightful trip through this small country that offers such a disproportionate quantity and quality of fascinating experiences.

The discovery that Peter and I travelled well together added to the snatches of hope I was collecting, and there was that conversation on Rhosili Down to cling to.

Chapter Ten

Bluebells and Wild Garlic

Carpeting moist areas in old deciduous woods, bluebells, when seen from a distance, create a colourful blue haze on hillsides and forest floors. Close-up, the many little delicate bells are like individual works of art.

The 'old deciduous woods' is significant in the case of Parc Mawr, where many non-native conifers were added in the 1960s. The area is now owned by the Woodland Trust, who are logging the conifers and replanting native ash, oak, birch, and beech in green plastic rabbit guards. At present there are some unsightly transitional areas, but it is well worth a visit as there is still much beauty. There are also things to be learned that won't be so obvious in a few years, such as our discovery that wild foxgloves appear to be the pioneer species when the land is cleared.

On Easter Monday, we returned to see the seasonal changes since the first time Peter had taken me there. Come with us for an afternoon walk in April and smell, hear, and see the delights of Parc Mawr:

The air is very fresh, without any trace of wood smoke or farm odours, even though we are looking down on a sheep farm. I like both these common local smells, but it's so invigorating to inhale deeply the pure freshness after a morning rain.

"What is that delicious, sweet smell?" I exclaim, and Peter leads me to a pile of freshly cut fir trees, still wet with rain. We agree that they smell like cooking homemade strawberry jam.

'The smell of wild garlic wafts on the breeze...'
Bluebells and wild garlic in Parc Mawr

Somewhat incompatible with jam, the smell of wild garlic wafts on the breeze, and we come upon masses of its white flowers, sometimes mingling with bluebells. For a while, the jam and garlic alternate, competing for attention, until we leave the recently logged area.

Birdsong is constant and varied, sometimes overlaid by the barking of a dog and even the crowing of a rooster in mid-afternoon. The bleating of lambs and ewes is almost as continuous as the singing of birds, as they try to pair up when disturbed by our presence on the other side of the fence. A pheasant, also upset by us, calls sharp warnings. Two crows, alarmed or angry or both, but not about us, sound plaintive as they chase a buzzard they may have thought was threatening their nest.

Brooks tumble and trickle down the hillside, adding cheerful sounds, as does the dripping of rain from trees after another shower. We add the cracking of twigs as we walk, and soon are surprised by other man-made sounds, although not in our woods. At first we take it to be distant thunder, but soon

63

Peter recognises it as the echoes of a barrage of shots and concludes that it is a clay-pigeon shoot somewhere in the valley. The shots echo six-fold from the surrounding hills. A shower, or perhaps tea-time, drives the guns away for a long spell, and we appreciate quietness from below and birdsong from above.

What else are we seeing besides bluebells, garlic, and forestry work? We are surrounded by green, green, and more green, as the native trees and shrubs are in varying stages of budding and leafing out. Those fresh, bright greens that are mostly lost in mature leaves are so pleasing now.

In the moister areas, the rocks and trees are covered with lush moss. Both gorse and broom add their bright yellows in drier places, and many little flowers such as anemone and violets add spots of colour. Two white cherry trees stand near each other but are the only two in bloom.

As we climb higher and come to sections where the side of the hill has been cleared, there are good views of the River Conwy snaking through the valley, backed by rolling hills. Soon we descend a steep hill and enter a stand of large, old, native oaks, a tiny remnant of the oak forests that used to cover the lower elevations of most Welsh hillsides many years ago. In *Protected Landscapes*, published by the Countryside Commission in 1987, we learned that in Snowdonia:

> Unusually for Britain, goats were one of the principal grazing animals and they are credited with the almost total destruction of the indigenous forest. In 1066 forest covered sixty per cent of the area; 900 years later it was reduced to three per cent.

Circling around, we come back to more beautiful carpets of bluebells near the end of our walk. The clouds break briefly and shafts of sunlight penetrate the woods, highlighting this scene that, more than any other, will always be springtime in Wales to me.

Chapter Eleven

Infinite Variety

At last I was to see the extensive moors I'd been craving. One morning in early May, we packed a picnic lunch and headed out for what became an eleven-hour, one-hundred-thirty-mile, circular drive through a part of Wales we'd never explored together.

After leaving the A5 just north of Pentrefoelas, we passed through the village where it is thought Abraham Lincoln's maternal great-great-grandparents lived. Intrigued by that fact and the unusual name, I had looked it up and learned that Ysbyty Ifan (Hospital of John) began in the late twelfth century as a subordinate community of the Knights of the Order of the Hospital of St. John of Jerusalem. Locally, the Knights provided help and sanctuary for travellers during war and lawless times. By the mid-1800s, their hospice site had been replaced by the parish church, and nothing remained of their establishment.

The Knights of St. John had begun in the late eleventh century in Jerusalem as monks treating sick pilgrims to the Holy Land, and then took on a military role in protecting pilgrims and captured territory during the Crusades. Forced to leave the Holy Land after the failure of the Crusades, they established themselves in Europe, having numerous bases in England. How long ago and far away that all seemed as we walked around the charming village that grew from the Knights' former base at Ysbyty Ifan.

In the high moors near the source of the River Conwy, I recalled another old book: *The River Conway* by Wilson MacArthur, 1952, which captures the feeling well:

> There is a sense of unreality, or of something transcending reality, about the lonely moors …

But how they must be transformed when the dark heather brightens and blooms!

The infant river flows from Llyn Conwy, nestling among the heather at an elevation of 1,488 feet. Where the road to Ffestiniog crosses over an old stone bridge, we scrambled down to look at the quaint little structure – the first bridge over the Conwy – all sharp angles and no arches, standing in stark isolation on these barren moors. As we absorbed the tranquillity of the scene, a skylark trilled overhead.

The river is only a couple of yards wide at this point, gently flowing around moss-covered stones before gathering pace and plunging over a waterfall into a small gorge and setting off on its journey of thirty miles to the sea. What adventures lie ahead as it winds its way across open moor land before crashing down Conwy Falls, through lovely Fairy Glen and on into the lower Conwy Valley? Always growing as it is joined by many tributaries, how many more bridges will it flow under before it yields itself to the Irish Sea?

A few miles beyond Pont Yr Avon-Gam, before joining the road from Trawsfynydd, we stopped to photograph a sweet little arched bridge with delicate ferns growing from its rustic stonework. Crossing a tiny stream that flows near the road, it carries an old grass track-way that appears to lead nowhere, its reasons for existing lost in the mists of time.

At our next stop, Peter told me the sad story of a place sacrificed for a city, reminding me of Yosemite National Park's Hetch Hetchy Valley and San Francisco in 1923. The village of Capel Celyn was flooded, when a dam was built in 1965 to create Llyn Celyn and add to Liverpool's water supply. The distinctive, plaintive cries of black-headed gulls, nearly as small as pigeons, seemed to echo the lament of *'Cofio Celyn'* (Remembering Celyn), which we saw daubed in large letters on a building nearby. Nothing of the village is now visible, only the remains of the old road leading down to the water's edge and disappearing into the lake.

Having stopped briefly for a look at the river Dee flowing from Bala Lake, we continued up over the moor-covered Berwyn Mountains as the morning's overcast sky broke out in windy showers. It was lunch time, so we ate our sandwiches in the car. By the time we had finished, sunshine illuminated the beautiful view across Cwm Rhiwarth.

Turning off at Llangynog, we made a side trip to Pennant Melangell, a lovely, narrow valley that penetrates into the mountains, with Blaen-y-Cwm waterfall spilling into its western end. Near St. Melangell's Church are several yew trees thought to be nearly two thousand years old. Surrounded by the ancient graveyard, the stone church, with its square tower at one end and rounded apse at the other, nestles beneath the bracken-covered mountains.

This fascinating church, built in the seventh century and rebuilt in the twelfth, was named for a young Irish woman who came to North Wales to lead a quiet, solitary life of prayer. In 604, after fifteen years without seeing another person, Melangell encountered a prince hunting hares, and in saving one of his quarry, she became the patron saint of hares. The prince, seeing her devotion and purity, gave the valley for a nunnery and declared hares a protected species. She lived there for another thirty-seven years, and her nunnery lasted long after her death.

Falling into disrepair in the 1950s, the church faced an uncertain future, until the necessary support was found to complete a proper renovation, which took from 1987 until 1992 to complete. Wonderfully restored, the church has an appealing lych gate entrance, and a fifteenth-century rood screen, put back to where it had stood for one hundred years before the Reformation, when such Roman Catholic features were removed from British churches.

The saint's stone shrine, made in the twelfth century, suffered the same fate, and after archaeological research uncovered the broken pieces, it was rebuilt in recent years. We loved this remarkable, historic church, in its remote, beautiful, and serene setting.

Passing through the charming village of Llanrhaeadr-ym-Mochnant, we drove up a busy, narrow road for nearly four miles to the highest waterfall in Wales. Pistyll Rhaeadr is often called the finest falls in Britain, and plunges 240 feet in a series of leaps, clothed on two sides by vegetation in a variety of textures and shades of green. A small footbridge offers the best vantage point for seeing the waterfall. Looking back at the whole scene from the road, we found only the top part of the falls visible, and the valley bathed in a gentle glow of late afternoon light.

Standing on a larger bridge, over the River Ceiriog, in the village of Llanarmon Dyffryn Ceiriog, we admired the way the slanting rays of the sun outlined a ewe drinking at the edge of the river. Looking at my quick snapshot of the scene reminds me that I couldn't refrain from teasing Peter a bit, when his usual painstaking setup cost him that shot. By the time he was ready, the ewe was walking away.

Our route home took us over the mountain road from Glyn Ceiriog to Llangollen. Winding and narrow in places, it passed through remote upland areas of grazing sheep, each accompanied by its ever-lengthening shadow as the evening sun fell lower in the sky. And there ahead of us in the distance we could see the sunlit ruins of Castell Dinas Bran standing prominently above the Dee valley.

Passing through Llangollen brought back poignant memories of my first trip to North Wales, in 1996, when I made a daytrip from Chirk to the famous eisteddfod town, before moving on to Conwy and that fateful meeting with Mona.

I quickly discovered that I had arrived at the Stanton House Hotel in Chirk on their monthly folk music night. This was my first real visit to Wales, and I was eager to hear some Welsh music, so I joined the group of seventeen in the dining room. In turn, each singer, mostly unaccompanied, sang a song of his or her choosing, with the group usually joining in on the chorus. When my turn came, not being a singer, I asked if I could tell a story instead, and they agreed. So I told them about my colleague and best friend at Sequoia National Park, who had come to Britain with me in 1990. In the intervening years we often spoke of a repeat trip, but I procrastinated while pursuing my own holiday goals for a few years. In the autumn of 1994, Anne became ill, and we lost her unexpectedly a month after her forty-fifth birthday.

"So the point of my story is this," I told the group of folksingers, "if there is any act of friendship or love in the back of your mind, do it now. We can't assume we have the luxury of doing things whenever we get around to it, because there are no guarantees in life."

They seemed to appreciate the story, and several spoke to me about Anne afterwards. I went to my room warmed by the thought that, for a few minutes on a cold winter night in North Wales, a group of strangers were thinking of Anne and the tragedy of her early death.

How often I thought of her during my long visits and wished I could tell her about having met Peter and the possibility of a future in Wales; she would have been so hopeful and excited for me.

The last stretch of our circular tour, in evening light, was full of sheep, pheasants, rabbits, and many large patches of bluebells, rounding out a memorable day.

'We admired the way the slanting rays of the sun outlined a ewe drinking…' Afon Ceiriog

Chapter Twelve

On Hearing the Cuckoo

Amidst intermittent showers, we walked the trail to Aber Falls with Tony and Gretta, at first staying near the musical little cascading river. The white flowers of the blackthorn were giving way to those of the hawthorn, and patches of bluebells created that lovely bluish haze on the hills as well as adding colour by the trailside. A swathe of yellow marsh marigolds alongside the river below the path was very eye-catching.

A small stone house and byre remain from an old farm, with the byre now housing interpretive displays. One of these was a large mural depicting local wildlife and land use over the centuries, and we looked for those creatures that had significance to us: chough, dipper, red kite, green woodpecker, mice, and badgers.

An eleven-acre, spring-fed alder woodland is another example of the history and industry of this area. Itinerant Welsh craftsmen used to make thousands of wooden soles here for local clog-makers. The alder coppice is still cut system-atically, and various stages of re-growth are visible, but now the wood is used for charcoal production, in kilns seen from the trailside.

We hoped at least to hear a cuckoo in the woods where I first heard one when Mona brought me here in 1999. Locals say spring actually begins when you hear the first cuckoo of the year, but we heard nothing of the elusive birds. I still stand by our bluebell experiences, though, as evidence of spring.

Afon Goch (Red River), eroding a path through shale, suddenly hit a 'dyke' of granite it couldn't cut through, forcing it to drop one hundred and fifteen feet over a rocky face to finish its short journey to the sea. Commonly known as Aber Falls, its Welsh name, Rhaeadr Fawr, means the Great Waterfall, and from this point the river assumes that name.

Rhaeadr Fawr is not the biggest in the country, but is called this in contrast to Rhaeadr Fach – the Little Waterfall, nearby. This little fall, narrower, but higher at two hundred feet, feels more remote and wild. A separate mountain stream creates Rhaeadr Fach but is soon lost in the water of Afon Rhaeadr Fawr, a quarter of a mile below the falls. Near the entrance of the valley, they join a third river, and their collective forces become Afon Aber.

Making a loop trip by returning over the hills on the west side of Rhaeadr Fach, we were rewarded with views of the mountains where these rivers begin, hidden from sight to walkers below. Tony and Gretta introduced us to this route, and looking up at the peaks and the scree-covered slopes plunging into the valley gave me a more alpine perception of this place. Continuing on through sheep pastures, looking down at the pretty, wooded river valley, we were soon gazing between heathery hills and headlands to the sea. As we approached the end, the sands of Traeth Lafan and Dutchman's Bank became visible, along with Puffin Island and Penmon Lighthouse, creating a wide, painterly scene of blue sky and sea and golden brown sand, with the green hills and bluebells at our feet.

Opposite: 'Known as Aber Falls, its Welsh name – Rhaeadr Fawr – means Great Waterfall.' The larger of the two falls at the top of Aber Valley

A path less travelled took us up Dulyn Valley in May. Nestled below Carnedd Llewelyn and Foel-fras, the high moor above the river valley was where we did finally hear the cuckoo. Leaving the plateau, we drove back down to where we could pick up a footpath to the Dulyn River. The setting among mossy boulders, marsh marigolds, and the bright green of young leaves was delightful, and we had the whole place to ourselves. We scrambled around on the rocks, trying various angles for photos of the river and the white ribbon of falling water flanked by lush vegetation.

The drive there and back was pretty as well, and I realized that bluebells and swallows, so notable when they first appeared, were now everywhere, including the verges of country roads.

How I should love to observe the seasons here without all the long breaks; to study the progression of bird arrivals and buds becoming blooms. To agree confidently with knowledgeable locals when they talk of spring being early or autumn coming late would be a pleasantly absorbing occupation for the rest of my days. Could it really come to pass?

Chapter Thirteen

Steal the Mountain

On a day while Peter was working, I took a bus to Blaenau Ffestiniog, to see the Llechwedd Slate Caverns. Wearing hard hats, we descended the incline deep into the caverns for a fascinating tour. Of thirty-two mines in the area one hundred years ago, only four are still operating, but slate roofing is making a comeback and keeping the industry alive. Formed of mud and clay compressed by granite, the slate in this area runs in veins dipping at thirty to thirty-five degrees. In other parts of Wales, the bands are horizontal or vertical. In all situations, the drilling for the insertion of explosives has to be at right angles to the veins. Teams of four, often consisting of family members, worked as a unit and shared the earnings: cutting large blocks from the wall by explosives; breaking them down and loading them onto carts for the mill; splitting to workable size; and dressing the slates to exact size and finishing them with deckled edges. Boys became apprentices at eight and regular workers at twelve; most men were forced to retire by thirty-five or forty, having contracted lung disease from the dust.

Sometime later, Peter, Tony, Gretta and I spent a grey day in a grey place and thoroughly enjoyed it. The Welsh Slate Museum at Llanberis, just outside Snowdonia National Park, at the foot of Mount Snowdon, also does an excellent presentation of the history of the slate industry. Two items in the introductory video stayed with me. It began with a quote from a labourer, "Steal a sheep from the mountain, and they hang you. Steal the mountain, and they make you a Lord."

Two men, one on either side of the mountain, became very rich from the hard and dangerous labour of local men and boys, while a government inquiry, turning a blind eye on lung disease, declared slate work to be "very healthy."

The second item was near the end of the story of the slate boom. One month after Prince Charles knelt on a huge, polished circle of slate for his investiture at Caernarfon Castle in 1969, this quarry that had produced the slate, was closed.

We walked all around the site, viewing with interest the huge water wheel, the workers' cottages, and a demonstration of splitting of slate.

In late May, Peter took me for a walk around a lake at Cwmorthin, a scenic valley partially marred by slate mining but retaining great natural beauty. Interspersed among the huge, glacially polished granite outcrops and the rugged cliff-topped hills stand large tips of slate waste. The scene is rendered more interesting by the ruins of the old mining buildings, their stonework intact, roofs and windows gone. Mostly housing for the workers, the ruins also include one large house, set well away from the others, a chapel, and a winding house on top of a hill. Only sheep make use of these buildings now, and we watched a ewe and lamb nibbling the grass in front of the hollow-eyed chapel. The bed of an old railway ran by the chapel, and we found one short stretch that still had a remnant of track. A long line of slate fencing divides the chapel area from the lake. This intriguing and attractive nineteenth century tradition utilises narrow, broken or rough-cut pieces of slate,

---

Opposite: 'Only sheep make use of these buildings now...'
Slate mine remains at Cwmorthin near Blaenau Ffestiniog

about three feet tall, wired together – an ingenious use of what may otherwise have been waste.

Peter made two evocative comments about Cwmorthin: "Imagine what this valley was like before there was any mining here;" and, "Imagine coming to work here on a glorious morning like this, and then going through that tunnel to spend the day underground, choking on slate dust."

Both were sobering thoughts.

There were lots of pied and grey wagtails, redstarts, and wheatears flitting about as we walked around the natural lake, where the edges are slowly being filled in by grasses. Wild orchids, cotton grass, and water lilies added colour, along with many other delicate, little pastel flowers nearly hidden in the grass.

Returning through Blaenau, we stopped for tea and ice cream. The young woman on a handsome little horse whom we'd passed alongside the road, arrived at the café while we were seated outside. I asked the girl if the horse had come for an ice cream, and she said, "Yes, mint with chocolate flake." Exactly what I was having!

Chapter Fourteen

Nesting Birds and Golden Rain

Peter's knowledge of little-known footpaths that are not part of a park or tourist site came in very handy during holiday weekends, when we chose to avoid crowded areas. Over the years of travelling in Britain, I have come to think of the footpath system as one of her most enlightened ideas, especially compared to the US, where many people are adamant about keeping private property strictly private.

Llysfaen, on the Sunday afternoon of May-Day weekend, was peaceful and lovely. The greener-than-ever hillsides, where we were alone with the sheep and the wind, seemed miles away from the string of coastal towns and resorts below us. There were numerous rugged limestone cliffs and country-side views in all directions. When we came to a cleft in the hills, the sight of the Irish Sea took me by surprise. It was here where we sat and watched rainbows, sometimes complete and double, over the hills opposite. They seemed a good omen to me.

Brilliant photos of South Stack lighthouse with a foreground of spring wildflowers grace guidebooks and maps of Anglesey and Wales. I longed to see it looking like that, but my first trip, made shortly before I went home in 2002, was too early for flowers, seabird breeding season, and tours of the lighthouse. I helped RSPB staff carry boxes of brochures and supplies down to the visitor centre at the lighthouse, and had a look around the reserve on a cold, grey day. Small numbers of seabirds were just beginning to nest on the cliffs that rise up to three hundred and sixty feet, and the ledges of the dramatic walls held mostly guillemots. Lesser black-backed gulls were the most visible, since they breed on the ground around the lighthouse. A peregrine falcon flew by as we walked the coast path, shiny black choughs darted about the cliff edge, and a hooded-crow looked for food in the grass.

The spectacular scenery includes eroded rocks along the coast, with sea caves and offshore 'stacks'. Looking back at the cliff face from the lighthouse, we saw crazily tilted, twisted and folded layers of sandstone, quartz and shale. A ferry on the foggy horizon was a reminder that the next land to the west is Ireland. The cries of gulls and the pounding of waves far below were the usual sounds, punctuated by the roar of helicopters and jets from RAF Valley.

Set back from the cliffs is a cluster of nineteen prehistoric hut circles from 2000 B.C., covering fifteen acres. The homes and agricultural buildings would have been made of stone and roofed with thatch. This wild, wind-swept environment seems an unlikely place to inspire thoughts of farming, but it must have worked for the Early Bronze Age settlers since the site was used for over a thousand years.

Fourteen months later, Peter and I managed to find the perfect combination of season, weather, and time off just days before the end of my two-month visit. Gorse and heather covered the cliff tops at the start of the walk, and smaller flowers made a patchwork of colours: pink thrift and yellow vetch being most common, blue spring squill, pink lousewort, and white pinks adding details. It was along this path that we had our best look at choughs, and we had frequent sightings of some of the local eleven pairs. The resident peregrine falcon I'd seen the previous year was sitting on a nest of sticks tucked into a rough niche in an otherwise smooth cliff-face.

This time, the ledges were full of noisy birds, which came and went between the sea and their nests. Seeing two puffins clearly through a powerful scope was very exciting for me; Peter was within a few feet of many puffins on Shetland some years ago, but I'd never seen any. South Stack is not a major puffin site, and as the guide who pointed them out said, "It's hard to find fifty puffins among three thousand guillemots and five hundred razorbills."

Numerous herring gulls and lesser black-backed gulls sat on their nests, surprisingly near the path, and were not disturbed by having people observe and photograph them.

Built in 1908 and still in use, the lighthouse sends out a beam every 10 seconds that can be seen for twenty miles. The small halogen bulb is housed in four-and-a-half tons of glass, brass, and cast iron, which turn on top of a frictionless bed of three-quarters of a ton of mercury. The walk to the lighthouse and climb to the top includes about six hundred and fifty steps and a short bridge across a narrow, one-hundred-foot-deep channel between the mainland and the small island that holds the lighthouse.

South Stack has such a variety of fascinating experiences to offer, I'll never tire of visiting there.

Bodnant Garden is a canvas on which new works of Nature's art appear throughout the spring, summer and autumn. Fields of daffodils, magnificent magnolias, camellias, rhododendrons, wisteria, and acres of azaleas grace the spring, but late-May and early-June's crowning glory is the laburnum arch. Its thousands of hanging golden blossoms have earned it the nickname 'Golden Rain', and the varied azaleas that border the arch complement the laburnum perfectly. The arch is alive with the buzzing of bees, and, unless you are the first visitors at the gate, as we were one memorable morning, it is equally buzzing with coach parties. Nevertheless, it is a sight not to be missed, regardless of the circumstances.

The Dell is my other favourite, where azaleas and rhododendrons flank the hillsides along the little River Hiraethlyn, which flows from the mill pond over a manmade waterfall. When the multi-coloured azaleas are in bloom, the view from the bridge above the falls is a treasure.

Even without flowers, the Garden boasts an amazing variety of trees, worth a visit in their own right. I am fortunate to have lived with both species of California redwoods: *Sequoiadendron giganteum*, 'Giant Sequoias', (I cannot bring myself to call them 'Wellingtonias') in Sequoia National Park, and *Sequoia sempervirens*, 'Coast Redwoods' in the San Francisco Bay area. I always enjoy Bodnant's specimens, all over a century old. They are well placed for visitors unfamiliar with them to study their differences. Also nearby is a fine specimen of the third type of redwood, the Dawn Redwood, originally native to China.

After several visits made at various times during two springs, it was easy to see why Bodnant is a garden of international significance.

Throughout my two-month trip, Peter was becoming more comfortable with the possibilities of a future together, and we had many wonderful times that spring. But my visit was not without a major setback. We recovered from that and were the stronger for it. A final battle with fear, he called it. By the time I left in late May, we were making tentative plans.

'The Dell, where azaleas flank the hillsides along the little River Hiraethlyn…' Bodnant Gardens in April

Chapter Fifteen

Ships in Harbour Are Safe

Sitting in the Departure Lounge at Manchester airport, we talked until the final call. Under discussion were Peter's holidays in July and October. We tentatively decided that he would come to see me in July, and, if all went well in the intervening months, we'd have an autumn wedding and honeymoon.

With no qualms of indecision this time, Peter prepared for his visit, and on the eleventh of July, I met him at the Philadelphia airport. The next day we went to a picnic where he met most of my large family: four siblings and their children and grandchildren. It was the first time since our Dad's funeral in 1998 that the five of us were together.

Returning to 'Philly' two days later, we headed for California, where I showed Peter some of my favourite places in Sequoia and Kings Canyon National Parks, and introduced him to old friends and former colleagues.

We wandered several trails among the giant trees; climbed to the top of Moro Rock for views of magnificent mountains; enjoyed the lush green meadows surrounded by Sequoias; admired the ingenuity of Tharp's Log (a summer dwelling in a fallen Sequoia log); cooled off beside cascading rivers; and were delighted with a fairly close sighting of a bear, spotted first by Peter. During a hike with two of my Park Service friends, he was impressed by views from the top of the cliff known as the 'Watchtower', and at Emerald Lake, experienced a very severe thunderstorm with lightning strikes all around. I had considered the possibility of driving to Yosemite National Park, farther north in the same mountain range, to show him the spectacular valley views and waterfalls, but we decided it was too far in the time we had. For really getting to know the Giant Sequoias and avoiding hordes of other visitors, I've always preferred Sequoia and Kings Canyon anyway, so it was a great pleasure to share them with Peter. He had wanted one more visit before we made a definite commitment. All went well, and we were both sure.

Immigration papers and fees, choosing what to take, what to ship, what to get rid of, and what to store in my sister's attic; planning farewell get-togethers with a wide variety of people; my mind was in a constant state of overload. Now it was my turn to feel the fear. How could I know for certain that he was really sure? Was his growing to love me as valid as falling in love? Some say it is more valid, but the romantic notion of 'falling in love' is well ingrained in the Western psyche. Whatever would I do if, after I gave up my new life and moved over there, things still fell apart? Legally, I had to be in Britain for twenty-two days before the wedding; what if, during those three weeks...? It didn't bear thinking about! But how could I, out of fear, say no to everything I had been dreaming of? I couldn't have lived with myself if I'd done that. All that I loved about being back in my hometown, near my family, and having my independence would have lost its glow if I only clung to it out of fear.

To sell my furniture and car, let my flat go, and ship my boxes before I left, I had to trust Peter and have faith that we were doing the right thing. We had often talked about our beliefs and having faith in the Plan for our lives, but my trust was never tried as much as during those weeks of burning bridges. Just before Peter's July visit I received a wonderful, welcoming letter from my future sister-in-law, Gwen. I was deeply touched and very encouraged by her thoughtful remarks.

Knowing that none of my family could attend the wedding, I asked my adult nieces who lived nearby to join me in shopping for a dress. I wasn't committed to having a dress from the US, but I thought I'd try one well-known shop in Ephrata, and if I didn't find what I wanted there, I'd wait and get one in Wales. After a variety of lovely things had been tried on and examined from all angles, we all agreed on an elegant, long dress and jacket in pale lilac. We celebrated over an equally elegant lunch afterwards.

As previously arranged, I e-mailed Gill, who had agreed to be my bridesmaid, and told her about the dress. I knew she had chosen a special suit for her son's summer wedding, and hadn't been able to wear it because of unusually hot weather, so I hoped she could wear it at our wedding. Soon photos of Gill modelling the suit and the dress she'd worn in its place arrived by e-mail, leaving me very surprised and disappointed that I had to tell her she still would not have an opportunity to wear the new suit. From the back, it looked so much like my outfit, I could scarcely believe it. We would have looked like two bridesmaids standing side by side wondering where the bride had gone!

Realising that Peter is not the type to wear anything the least bit formal, I encouraged him to wear the handsome tweed jacket he had had specially made by a local seamstress on Castle Street. During a wonderful fortnight on Harris in the summer of 2002 with two college friends from Stoke-on-Trent, Peter had purchased a length of tweed directly from a weaver, and the resulting jacket suited him perfectly. It was also perfect for the sort of wedding we planned, and the country setting of our reception.

'The great day came – 11 October 2003 – and we loved every detail as we saw our plans unfold.'

Immigration, shipping, my flight, and those three weeks of wedding preparations in Conwy, all went smoothly, reassuring us in every way.

The great day came – Eleventh October 2003 – and we loved every detail as we saw our plans unfold. "Bind us together with cords that cannot be broken; Bind us together with love," the congregation sang, as I walked down the short aisle of St. John's Methodist Church. The guests from afar, people whom I hadn't previously met, included a Scot from South Uist who had worked with Peter in Shetland twenty years before, and five friends from University days, who hadn't all been together in thirty years. We were sorry Peter's cousin Lynn was unable to join us, but her invitation to visit them in France soon after the wedding was an exciting consolation. Feeling warmly welcomed, I didn't waste a minute on homesickness or sadness at having no family or old friends of my own there. I knew they were with us in spirit, and I looked forward to telling them about it and sending photos.

It may seem odd to choose a bridesmaid from among such new friends, but if you knew Gill, you would understand that sometimes a new friend can feel just as appropriate and supportive as a friend of many years. Peter had introduced us at church during my first visit, but we had not spent much time together. As Gill and I donned our wedding attire in her home, her calmness and spiritual depth reassured and strengthened me.

We were escorted to church by Roy, also a friend from St. John's, who had believed this wedding would take place ever since Peter introduced me. He and his wife and 'life-support system', Brenda, had encouraged me whenever I lost hope. I had asked him to walk me down the aisle, and, as I gripped his arm, I couldn't help thinking how fortunate their daughters are.

The weather was made to order: dry and bright, but not too blinding for outdoor portraits, and the only still day in a windy week or more.

The reception for sixty-five guests was delightful and the food, delicious. Tony's droll humour as Best Man was enjoyed by all as he read a poem of his own composition for the toast:

> Now Peter Jones instead of the pub,
> Did much prefer the Camera Club.

Thus it began, to everyone's delight. Peter thanked his brother and sister-in-law for their support and told the story of my having met Mona, who was sitting at the head table. Nearby was a framed photo of Gwilym who had died between my two long visits. If he'd still been alive, I'd have wanted him to be there, too.

Peter hadn't been to see old friends from his year of living in the Lake District for a long time, so we went to Eskdale for our honeymoon. Our self-catering stay in a converted barn, with no one around but the owners in the nearby house, was perfect for getting away from it all. Boot, where he'd lived, was charming, and I enjoyed meeting his friends around the area.

We returned from our honeymoon to find we were minor local celebrities. Rhodri from Camera Club (the young man on the phone who'd encouraged me to crash their party in 2001 and who also took the photos at our wedding) had asked if he could do a press release about our having met at the club, to show that it also has a social side. We said yes. The day before the wedding, a reporter rang and interviewed Peter about our meeting. When we came out of the church a news photographer awaited us, and the local weekly used a colour photo on the front page, although the photo used was actually taken by one of our Camera Club friends. Now we know what it feels like to be "Full story on page two" subjects. It was fun to receive congratulations on the street, in the library and shops, and for Peter, on the buses. Since Peter was considered a perennial bachelor, there was much interest in his finally getting married, and I am still in awe of the fact that it should be me he married!

Chapter Sixteen

And a Heron
at the Bottom of the Garden

My new home is on the edge of Conwy, bordered by rural properties on three sides. It is all the more special to me, knowing how the house came to be, after Peter returned home from fifteen years of working in various parts of Britain. Helped by his brother, who can turn his hand skilfully to almost any trade, and encouraged by their Dad, who was still making the tea when he was nearly ninety, Peter had spent most of his spare time for ten years building this house on part of the land adjoining the family home. He moved in on his birthday in 1996, and his father lived with him for four years before going into a nursing home where he died at the age of ninety-five in the summer of 2002.

Old and new, town and country, these contradictions are the best way to characterize the setting of our house. Cattle graze the fields directly across the road from us, and sheep munch the grass on the other side of the stream that forms our back boundary. It is this stream at the bottom of the garden that provides the scenes that thrill me most: a heron standing for hours, watching for fish and eels, or sometimes sunbathing, or in early morning, hunting mice and slugs in our field. Its majestic flight when startled always makes me catch my breath in awe.

Once, during a sudden, heavy afternoon hailstorm we hurried to the big window in the sitting room to watch the hailstones, and were surprised to see the heron literally running for cover to his favourite fishing spot by a tree-covered bend in the river. There he hunkered down and waited out the storm. On another occasion he put on quite a dramatic show for us, grappling with a large eel. Since this most agile fish can wrap itself around a heron's beak or neck, catching and getting an eel down can be a tricky manoeuvre. We were relieved to see 'our heron' succeed after a long struggle.

Living close to Nature is important to both of us, and I am thrilled to think that I will always have the pleasures of the gardens Peter created before I arrived, complete with rockery, hedges, stone walls, small field, and stream, which invite many little creatures to share our place. On clear days, we see a few of the peaks of Snowdonia, and Tal-y-Fan, the most northerly in the range, is our nearest, only two miles away. Now, I am in Wales to stay year-round; to watch the play of cloud shadows on the mountains, to observe the progression of blackthorn, bluebells, buttercups, foxgloves, hawthorn berries, and that most longed-for sight, the moors turning purple.

Occasionally, during our first months of marriage, I mentioned to Peter that I'd like to have a dog when we felt ready for it, but I warned him that my pets have always found me, and not necessarily at what seemed the ideal time. One day, Maldwyn, a colleague of Peter's, stopped by for a visit on his way home from a long bicycle trip and mentioned that his neighbours needed to find a new home for the nine-month-old dog they'd bought for their two little girls at Christmas. The strong little dog had become too much for them and their small yard. In reply to Maldwyn's asking if we were interested, we said we weren't ready. A week passed, and he rang during our breakfast to say that he and Margaret had 'Jack' for the day, and asked if they could bring him over for us to see him. To my surprise, knowing how much harder it would be to turn a dog away once we'd met him, Peter said yes. Needless to say, Jack never left and quickly wormed his way into our hearts and lives.

He's a mongrel, probably half Welsh Corgi. His lovely golden-brown colour, white patch on his chest and toes, and his pointy ears make him quite handsome. His brown eyes are soft and gentle. The name 'Jack' seemed too plain for him, and we wanted to call him something else, but we wanted to keep the sound similar so as not to confuse him. We tried 'Jock' but we both preferred a name with two syllables, since that's what we were used to. 'Jocan' (JOCK-kan) was the result, a unique name for a unique dog. He can run like the wind, looking like a tiny greyhound when in motion; our half-acre must seem like heaven to him. Indoors, he is as sweet a lapdog as I've ever known; outdoors, he is a complete tearaway, causing Peter to give him the nickname 'Jocan and Hyde.'

We began taking him with us as much as possible, and I decided to try him on a short bus trip to town; if he could ride the buses with me, we could vary the starting points of our walks while Peter was at work. Wanting to stop at the Castle Street chemist before we headed for the Marine Walk, I tied Jocan to the big, wrought-iron gates at the entrance to the churchyard. A woman we'd met during our wedding preparations was waiting at the counter, and we exchanged greetings.

"How's your puppy?" she asked.

I thought Peter must have told her about the addition to our family, so I said,

"He's fine; I've just tied him to the churchyard gates while I pick up my photos."

She just stared at me oddly and said nothing. I desperately tried to think what I'd said wrong, and then it hit me.

"Did you say, 'How's your hubby?'"

Of course she had, so I explained about Jocan. I never use

the word 'hubby', and so it hadn't entered my mind. I couldn't wait to tell my 'Dear *Gŵr*' that night, and for days we laughed every time we recalled the image of Peter tied to the churchyard gates.

For my birthday the year before, Peter had sought out a copy of an old book he'd read years ago and gave it to me. *I Bought a Mountain* by Thomas Firbank (first published in 1940) gave me my first glimpse into the life of the hill farmer and deepened my appreciation for the remote farms and old ruins that we see during our excursions. Later, in one of my frequent searches through the 'Wales' section of Conwy's High Street antiquarian bookstore, I stumbled onto Elizabeth West's *A Hovel in the Hills* (1977), packed with information and country charm. In moving to Peter's house, I realised I would not be living the type of life described in these old books, but at the age of fifty-nine and with a background of fairly soft living, I knew Peter's lifestyle was the perfect compromise for me.

Learning to use his solid-fuel Rayburn for cooking, baking, heating the house and water, and drying the laundry on an overhead rack has been challenging, and mostly pleasurable. Coming into the warm kitchen on a cold, wet, or windy day is as homely as anything I've ever experienced. There is plenty of scope for me to feel a sense of adventure in adapting to life in a different country and climate, and there is always something new to learn.

British people often ask me, with gloomy overtones, how I like the climate here. They're usually surprised when I say it is one of the attractions for me. Pennsylvania's extremes of winter cold and summer heat and humidity are less appealing now than they were in childhood. And California's sunny Mediterranean climate, perpetually pleasing to most people, had become too much of a good thing after thirty years. I like changeable weather, wind, rain and interesting cloud effects, frost and, occasionally, a little snow, unpredictable temperatures, but rarely too hot or too cold. North Wales, between the mountains and the sea, suits me perfectly.

Life with Peter is a tapestry rich in the colours and textures of the landscapes, weather, and wildlife of North Wales. The pattern also includes a few more Welsh words and the thrill of achieving the goal I'd set for myself at the Town Band concert that first Christmas: joining in the enthusiastic singing of the Welsh National Anthem at the close of an Aled Jones concert, with mistakes and a terrible accent, I'm sure. Singing it while holding hands with a Welshman was a bonus I never even imagined back then.

Gratitude is the loom on which this varied tapestry of our new life together is woven, and I feel a surge of it every time I answer the question, "Are you on holiday?"

'I warned Peter that my pets have always found me, and not necessarily at what seemed the ideal time.'

dinas

For more information about this innovative imprint,
contact Lefi Gruffudd at lefi@ylolfa.com or go to
www.ylolfa.com/dinas.
A Dinas catalogue is also available.